MISS CARSTAIRS
DRESSED FOR BLOODING

Signature Series

MISS CARSTAIRS
DRESSED FOR BLOODING

and other plays
by

PETER REDGROVE

Marion Boyars
London

A MARION BOYARS BOOK
distributed by
Calder and Boyars Ltd
18 Brewer Street, London W1R 4AS

This volume first published in Great Britain in 1977
by Marion Boyars Publishers Ltd
18 Brewer Street, London W1R 4AS

ISBN 0 7145 2556 1 Cased edition
ISBN 0 7145 2557 X Paper edition

Miss Carstairs Dressed for Blooding is adapted from an incident in
The Terrors of Dr Treviles by Peter Redgrove and Penelope Shuttle
published in 1974 by Routledge & Kegan Paul.

In the Country of the Skin is a radio play adapted from
Peter Redgrove's novel of that name published in 1973 by
Routledge & Kegan Paul.

Three Pieces for Voices was originally published in 1972 by
Poet & Printer.

Printed in Great Britain by
Unwin Brothers Limited,
The Gresham Press, Old Woking, Surrey
A member of the Staples Printing Group

MISS CARSTAIRS DRESSED FOR BLOODING

A GHOST STORY FOR TELEVISION

MISS CARSTAIRS DRESSED FOR BLOODING

DR GREGORY TREVILES: Fiftyish, well-preserved, bearded, tall

DR BRIDGET HARE: Early thirties, a little under average height, intense, brainy, hot-tempered, slightly masculine in manner and dress

MYSTERIOUS COUPLE: They resemble BRID and GREGORY quite closely. The chief difference is that they behave with more glee. Perhaps played by the same actors as the above

KIOSK LADY: Unremarkable, plump, forties, dressed in ordinary overall, hair dressed so that ears are visible

MISS CARSTAIRS: Remarkable appearance, commanding, waved iron-grey hair, late sixties, upperclass day-clothes, firm clear educated voice

BRID and GREGORY *in bed. Their relationship is in the doldrums.* BRID *is over-sensitive, jumpy, probably pre-period jumpiness and tension.* GREGORY's *attempts to make love are irritating her, though he is a practised lover. It is because of her over-sensitivity, though she wants to make love more than anything. They lie in the rumpled bed. Sunlight shines through the windows.*

GREGORY: And my rod and my staff shall comfort you.

BRID: Well they don't.

> *She sits up in bed and lights a cigarette with an angry gesture.* GREGORY *is irritatingly calm. His calm hides his own irritation, which is liable to flash out.* BRID *is ready to take it out on* GREGORY, *and he is ready to rise to her bait.*

BRID: You've lost your healing touch, **Doctor** Treviles.

GREGORY: My touch? And you your relenting skin, Brid.

BRID: Your bedside manner. The Treviles Bed-In. The Treviles Laugh-In!

GREGORY: Balls. Come here Brid. Doctor to Doctor. Healer to Healer.

BRID: Come to heel? Curate to curate. Let us pray!

GREGORY: It **is** supposed to be a holiday.

BRID: Our last chance together you mean, the cure, like taking the cure, Healer. What cure, Lover.

GREGORY: You're over-reacting again, Brid.

7

BRID: Don't you talk to me about symptoms. I'm
a doctor too. If I say I'm feeling fine I'm feeling fine.
Brains don't count here.

GREGORY: Brains count anywhere. Bed included.

BRID: I'm not frightened of you, Gregory Treviles.

GREGORY: You're not frightened of anybody, Bridget.
That's your trouble. You never give in.

BRID: I'll give in to anybody who's worth giving in to.

*They are both sitting up in bed, tense, frowning and
angry. The glum couple contrasts with the sunny
windows, which the camera shows us, perhaps with
some titles; moves back to bed. Some time has passed.
BRID's cigarette is finished. They lie with heads
propped up on the pillows, GREGORY on our left,
BRID on our right. They doze uncomfortably, with
closed eyes. GREGORY speaks suddenly, but as if
in his sleep.*

GREGORY: Give me the map Brid.

*BRID is startled and her eyes snap open. What map?
She turns to the bedside table but it is empty save for
a lamp, she looks in the drawer of the table. No map.*

GREGORY: GIVE ME THE MAP BRID.

*Now there is a transition to the couple in their open
car. The change-over emphasizes the similarity of
their positions in the car to their positions in bed, as by
showing them one moment in bed, the next moment in
bed in their car-clothes, the next moment going along in
the car naked or in night-clothes, the next moment in bed*

8

*with the sunny countryside streaming past as though
they were in the open car, the next moment sitting
up in the car in the bedroom — at the last, however,
driving along in their open tourer through the
sunshine and the green country. The car is
a distinctive old tourer, ideally an early 'Bullnose'
Morris.*

GREGORY: Give me the map Brid.

BRID *reaches forward to the glove compartment and
finds the map. She offers it to* GREGORY *but his
eyes are on the road.*

GREGORY: Read it for me Brid.

BRID *puzzles over the map.*

BRID: Where are we Gregory. I can't find where we are.

GREGORY *tries to squint over to look at the map.
It's too difficult so he pulls the car up to the grass
verge of the country road.*

GREGORY: I'm afraid we're lost.

BRID: Oh bloody hell. You shouldn't have brought us
so far.

GREGORY: You wanted to come.

BRID: It was your suggestion in the first place.

GREGORY: Will you stop taking it out on me!

BRID: Taking it out on you. I like that!

9

GREGORY: You may as well like it. There's nothing
          I can do until I find a signpost. So shut up. Please.
          Please shut up.

          *The sun goes in as he says PLEASE SHUT UP. He
          puts the car in gear but it has begun to rain. He pulls
          up again and starts to get out.*

BRID: What are you doing now?

GREGORY: Dear Brid, it's beginning to rain and if
          I don't put the hood up you'll get soaked and you
          know how you love that.

          GREGORY *walks to the back of the car and starts
          to loosen the hood in order to pull it over. It works
          all right on his side but on* BRID's *it is stuck.
          He struggles with it.*

BRID: Hurry up Gregory it's beginning to rain and I'm
          cold.

GREGORY: I should shay sho.

BRID: What was that!

GREGORY: I should say you are cold.

BRID: You Bastard... keeping your cool at all costs... cold,
          old bastard... you're so **old** Gregory... nothing ever
          cures anno domini — nothing ever heals that... only old
          Doctor Death... can you feel his old cold breath over
          your shoulder, Doctor Treviles?

          A gust of cold rain. BRID's *speech is the last straw
          for both of them.* GREGORY *raises his hand across
          the top of the car door to strike* BRID. *This will be*

10

a whopper, his hand is drawn right back. Freeze.
Remainder of titles perhaps...
GREGORY's *hand begins to descend across picture*
in such a manner as to allow us to see up the road,
in the direction from which BRID *and* GREGORY
have travelled. In the distance, a familiar-looking car
is approaching, quite fast. As it nears us we see that
the car is indeed an identical model, and the couple
in it are dressed exactly like BRID *and* GREGORY.
Their faces too are very similar — except that there is
more glee in these faces. As they pass the parked car
they wave gleefully at BRID *and* GREGORY, *tooting*
the horn cheerfully. GREGORY's *surprise turns his*
intended blow into a puzzled wave to the passing car.

BRID: Did you see that!

GREGORY: They looked exactly like us!

BRID: Who on earth were they? Who could they be?

GREGORY: There's only one way of finding out. Brid,
let's follow them.

BRID: Their car was the same too — **exactly** like ours.

GREGORY: We must follow them and speak to them.
We're lost anyway so there's nothing to lose.

He gets back into the car and starts it up. The
astonishment BRID *and* GREGORY *felt has turned*
into pleased excitement. Both have forgotten the
hood, which lies back unheeded. They have another
purpose now, and though the weather is overcast,
they no longer feel the few spots of rain a threat.
They drive off in hot pursuit...
Brief chase. BRID *and* GREGORY *almost catch up,*

*then fall back. Overhead shots. Then suddenly there
is an empty road. The pursuers are puzzled. They
brake, and look around. There is a driveway with
stone pillars set back from the road, and a notice
which says:* CARSTAIRS HOUSE AND GROUNDS
OPEN TO THE PUBLIC.

GREGORY: This is the way.

BRID: Come on Gregory we'll lose them.

*He turns the car, passing by the notice. He glances
at it, and we see as if through his eyes:* CARSTAIRS
HOUSE AND GROUNDS OPEN TO THE PUBLIC.
Now we see it, looking past GREGORY, *as if through*
BRID's *eyes, and to her it says:* CARSTAIRS
HOUSE AND GROUNDS OPEN TO DR GREGORY
TREVILES M.D. AND DR BRIDGET HARE M.B.,
B.S. FOR ONE HALF-HOUR ONLY. *She is startled,
and rubs her eyes. The letters reform to* CARSTAIRS
HOUSE AND GROUNDS OPEN TO THE PUBLIC
ON THURSDAYS ONLY NO BITCHES ALLOWED.
*She is left staring back over her shoulder at the
strange notice-board...*
*The weather is still threatening and very overcast.
There is a spatter of rain as they draw up on the
gravel in front of the house. It is a Georgian mansion,
built about 1770.* BRID, *afraid of getting wet, sprints
for the porch.* GREGORY *again tries to free the car's
hood, but gives up and also scampers for shelter.
The day is quite darkened with rain. The pair
examine the front door of the house. Its lintel is
supported by caryatids that have a distinctive face,
a woman's face that shows a masculine strength.
It has short, waved hair cut in the stone. This is a face
that* GREGORY *and* BRID *will become very familiar
with. It is the* CARSTAIRS *face...*

12

*There is a brass doorknocker, a large one, in the shape
of a horse's head.*

BRID: I'll knock shall I?

BRID *reaches up to the doorknocker and as her hand
approaches it, it changes to the living head of a horse
which bares its teeth and whinnies at her. She
snatches her hand back.* GREGORY *doesn't appear
to notice. He reaches for the handle of the door,
turns it.*

GREGORY: Look Brid, the door's open.

*They walk into the domed entrance hall. There is
a good broad staircase, and there are long windows
to one side. Sun shines through these, quite ignoring
the black and overcast day from which* BRID *and*
GREGORY *have just stepped. To one side of the
door there is a small kiosk with postcards and
a ticket machine worked by a woman attendant.
At the top of the staircase the couple whom they
have been chasing, dressed just like them, have paused,
the woman looking back over her shoulder, grinning
with glee. The next instant they are gone.* GREGORY
and BRID *move forward to follow, but the woman in
the kiosk interrupts.*

KIOSK LADY: Tickets please.

GREGORY: We haven't got tickets yet.

BRID: Can we buy them here?

KIOSK LADY: Children half price.

GREGORY: There's just ourselves. Just two. How much?

KIOSK LADY: Children under twelve half price. Age of descent. Have you got a dog, Sir?

GREGORY: No, just the two of us.

KIOSK LADY: One and a half, Sir. No tantrums allowed. No bitches. They chase the horses, you see.

GREGORY: Two adults. Just two adult tickets please.

KIOSK LADY: That will be fifty pence. Thank you, Sir. Thank **you**, Madam.

The KIOSK LADY *clearly doesn't approve of* BRID. *The latter doesn't know whether to be pleased at being offered a child's ticket, or offended at the pointed mention of lady dogs. Meanwhile, the couple at the head of the stairs have disappeared, and* GREGORY *is anxious to be after them.* BRID *is a little more reluctant, and lingers as if to question the* KIOSK LADY, *but the latter turns her head abruptly away.* BRID *sees that there is a thick tuft of hair growing on the point of the* KIOSK LADY's *ear, gives a little shriek, and catches up with* GREGORY.

They climb the staircase and reach the landing. Just as a few minutes earlier they surveyed a road empty of the elusive couple, now they confront an empty corridor. The corridor is lined with showcases full of objects, dress-dummies wearing ancient costume, pictures and weapons fastened to the panelled walls. Far away, at the end of the corridor, is a long sunlit window. Now it is GREGORY's *turn to hesitate, but* BRID *is fascinated by this corridor and its contents, and moves dreamily down it, lingering over the objects on display. The first part of the corridor is devoted to objects of a light colour, such as cradles,*

christening clothes, a child's toys and horn-books,
and at the end of this first part there is a dress-dummy
wearing an old wedding-gown, labelled MISS
CARSTAIRS' WEDDING-DRESS. *The second part*
of the corridor is devoted to objects of a sombre or
black hue: bibles, account books, ebony statuettes,
dark bronzes, sombre overcast landscapes, and at
the end of this second part of the corridor is a dress-
dummy wearing a black dress and jet beads labelled
MISS CARSTAIRS' MOURNING-DRESS. *The third*
part of the corridor contains objects of a martial or
sporting nature, and the hue is predominantly red.
There are weapons, sporting prints, fox-brushes,
riding-crops, scarlet uniforms, military helmets,
pistols, swords, and at the end of this section, near
the sunlit window, is a dress-dummy wearing hunting
pink and labelled MISS CARSTAIRS' HUNTING-
DRESS. *The* CARSTAIRS *name and the*
CARSTAIRS *face infest this corridor, its pictures*
and its showcases. There are cameos, portraits, old
photographs, and all have the same face, which is also
the face of the caryatids we have already seen
supporting the lintel of the house's front door. It is
the same whether the picture purports to be that of
a man, or that of a woman. In the men's portraits,
the men have a feminine emphasis, as though it were
a woman in man's clothes, and when it is the portrait
of a woman, the head is somewhat masculine, as
though she were in drag. But it is the same face
throughout, as though, through the ages, there were
only this one person...
Some of the objects, especially in the hunting section,
are very unusual, as for instance a crucifix of
MISS CARSTAIRS, *naked, the same* CARSTAIRS
face in agony, pierced hands and feet, with a label
reading CRUCIFIX REPLICA OF MISS CARSTAIRS
PRESENTED TO THE COMPANIONS OF

PERSEPHONE. *As* BRID *looks at this exhibit, she might notice that it seems just alive, with a small movement of the breasts as if just breathing, and the eyelids flickering as if about to open... BRID drifts up the corridor, excited and attentive to the exhibits. GREGORY is more interested in finding the couple who vanished, and he tries several locked doors, lagging behind BRID, who has disappeared at the end of the corridor, into the sunlight from the window there. Then we hear her voice calling. This corridor-walk very much lessens the tension between the couple, and the exciting oddity of its contents begins the* detente *between them.*

BRID: Gregory? Gregory?? Gregory!

GREGORY *hurries up the corridor and, passing also into the sunlight, finds BRID contemplating a portrait hanging to the right of the sunlit window. The portrait shows the same window, but giving on to a dark thundery landscape. Across the painted clouds slashes a jagged flash of lightning. MISS CARSTAIRS is painted standing to the right of this same window, but as a young woman, without the disturbing ambisexual look of the other portraits we have seen. She is radiant. In her left hand she holds the bridle of a little horse. In her right hand, the one nearest the window, she holds the severed brush of a fox. On her forehead is a bright smear of blood. The picture, which is recognizably of the same panelled interior in which BRID and GREGORY are standing, is labelled MISS CARSTAIRS DRESSED FOR HUNTING.*

BRID: I love this picture, Gregory. Look, Miss Carstairs has obviously been blooded on her first hunt. There's the fox's brush, the tail they cut off and gave to her.

There's the proud smear of blood they brushed on to
her forehead to show she had been good in the hunt.
The Master of Fox Hounds would have done this
himself. There's the horse she rode. And perhaps
that's the thunderstorm she rode through, which
makes her especially brave, over those drenched fields
and woods and meadows after the cunning fox.

GREGORY: I can't see the blood of a hunted animal
without a shiver, Brid, even after all the blood I've
seen as a Doctor. I feel I'm dedicated to healing, not
the shedding of blood.

BRID: I don't know that there can be a cure without
the shedding of blood. Once doctors always drew
a basin of blood from their patients' veins, whatever
the disease. Or they applied leeches to suck blood,
to draw off the humours.

GREGORY: Medicine is a science now...

BRID: No, Gregory, it's still an art. An art like the art
of painting. I love this picture. Can't you see how
gorgeous it is... it's **bloody** gorgeous, Gregory.

GREGORY: Well, it's a Gainsborough, if that's what you
mean. MISS CARSTAIRS DRESSED FOR HUNTING
by Thomas Gainsborough 1727-1788, according to
the label.

BRID: Will they let us photograph it? Have you got your
camera in the car?

GREGORY: I'm sure they've got postcards at that kiosk
downstairs...

BRID: Let's go down there now, Gregory. I don't care

what else there is, I must have a picture of this to take home. Gregory? I must have a picture. I won't leave without one. Gregory, are you coming?

BRID *walks off down the corridor, back the way they have come, and* GREGORY *is left staring after her...*
GREGORY *is approaching the top of the staircase, and before he can see her, he hears* BRID *arguing with the* KIOSK LADY.

KIOSK LADY: There's no need to take that tone with me, **Madam**. I'm sure I don't know where the blood has gone. I don't know where the lightning-flash is.

Both BRID *and the* KIOSK LADY *are holding copies of postcards. They are arguing across a litter of postcards on the top of the kiosk counter.*

BRID: But where has the blood gone, then? Where is the lightning? Here's the picture, and it's a nice large colour postcard, but there's no blood on the girl's forehead, and no lightning out of the window!

GREGORY *walks up behind* BRID *and looks over her shoulder. We see that the postcard is identical to the portrait* MISS CARSTAIRS DRESSED FOR HUNTING *upstairs, except that the girl's forehead has no smear of blood on it, she holds a riding-crop instead of a bloody fox's brush in her right hand, and the great flash of lightning is missing from the landscape shown by the long window.*

GREGORY: Brid! It must be another picture. It's not this lady's fault.

KIOSK LADY: Don't blame me Madam. I don't know

18

where the blood has gone. Or the lightning. Or the fox's tail. There's only one picture so far as I know. There's only this postcard.

GREGORY: I wouldn't have thought there'd be two pictures like this both by Gainsborough.

BRID: Look. In the picture upstairs. It's called MISS CARSTAIRS DRESSED FOR HUNTING. And clearly labelled by Thomas Gainsborough seventeen something to seventeen something. Well, somehow she's got her horse indoors into the panelled gallery upstairs for the painter, and she's got this big window over her right shoulder, and a great blue jagged flash or lightning outside the window, and she's got a red fox's tail in her right hand, here, where this riding crop is, and she's been painted with this smear of blood on her brow, here, on her forehead. Gregory?

KIOSK LADY: Just like the postcard in your hand, Madam.

BRID: Except for the blood. And the lightning. Gregory, where's the lightning-flash?

GREGORY: Maybe it's another picture, Brid.

BRID: But **this** postcard is clearly labelled on the back MISS CARSTAIRS DRESSED FOR HUNTING by Thomas Gainsborough 1727-1788 and there's no indication that there's another picture, and I want a postcard of the one with the blood and the lightning. I want the lightning and the blood on my postcard just as it is on the picture we saw upstairs so can I see the Curator please?

KIOSK LADY: He's out with the hunt.

19

BRID: What did you say?

KIOSK LADY: He's not here today.

BRID: I'll see his assistant then. Or anybody. Gregory!

KIOSK LADY: I'm the only one here. I ought to have given you half-price for tantrums of course.

BRID: What? WHAT did you say!

KIOSK LADY: I said it's nice outside you should see the little horse.

BRID: The only horse I want to see is the one on the postcard and Miss Carstairs with her fox's tail and her lightning out of the window and her first blood on her head.

MISS CARSTAIRS: I am Miss Carstairs. Let me help.

This new voice interrupts the quarrel with confident resonance.

MISS CARSTAIRS: Let me help.

It is the face of all the portraits, the CARSTAIRS face. This representative of it is a lean intelligent gynander in her sixties. GREGORY and BRID are startled by the interruption and turn round to face her as she descends the stairs.

GREGORY: Miss Carstairs? I — I don't understand.

MISS CARSTAIRS: The little girl in the picture was my great great great grandmother. Gainsborough stayed in this house when he was at the height of his career.

20

That was exactly two hundred years ago, in 1774, the
year he moved from Bath to the greater city of
London. He stayed here, and he painted Miss
Carstairs in her maiden triumph as a young rider to
hounds. The picture is insured for fifty thousand
pounds. Would you like a postcard of it?

BRID: Yes, please, I would very much like a postcard,
Miss Carstairs, but would you be so kind as to tell me
why the postcards you are selling for fifteen p. show
neither the blood on your ancestor's forehead nor
the lightning flash out of the window, why is there no
blood or lightning in the picture, Miss Carstairs, do
you think it is quite fair at the price Miss Carstairs?

MISS CARSTAIRS: Why of course I'll tell you, with
pleasure, Dr Hare. Blood and lightning would frighten
the little horse.

GREGORY *and* BRID *are nonplussed by* MISS
CARSTAIRS' *unexpected knowledge of* BRID's
*name, and neither much like her explanation, which
sounds too much like a sneer at their expense.*

BRID: Miss Carstairs...

GREGORY: Miss Carstairs, if you think you're being
funny Miss Carstairs, let me tell you that my fiancée
and I are not amused. We came here in good faith and
enjoyed the pictures and the atmosphere and the
objects on view and all we asked was to be allowed
to do so without interference and to return home
with some small memento of our visit such as an
accurate photograph or postcard of an exhibit
we particularly enjoyed and now there seems to be
something inaccurate and shady and possibly not
quite legal about your postcards of an important

21

painting I for one have never heard of as if you were
trying to persuade us to buy something we didn't
quite want because you've got some left over and on
top of it all I find it quite suspicious that you seem
to know our names and who we are.

MISS CARSTAIRS: You make your feelings quite plain
to me, Dr Treviles.

GREGORY: Do you see what I mean? She knows my
name too.

MISS CARSTAIRS: And I sympathize with your
feelings, Gregory, for I know there is something
lacking from your life which Brid Hare almost gave
you. And I know there is something lacking from
Brid Hare's life which could descend on you both
like a ray of sunlight or a drenching storm or a flash
of lightning or a pack of hounds to tear you to
pieces...

GREGORY: Now that is **it**, Miss Carstairs. We did not
come here to your peculiar and egoistic house where
everybody seems to wear your face to be told our
fortunes in the cut-glass accents of the over-privileged
remnant of Tory land-owning classes, but YES talking
about lightning and dogs my fiancée and I would like
that reminiscence or keepsake we spoke of to remind
us of the **pleasant** part of our visit and as I believe
you are legally obliged to sell us goods on show as
these postcards are, we will take one postcard thank
you very much and here is twenty p. and please keep
the change.

MISS CARSTAIRS: Physicians, heal thyselves.

GREGORY: Come, Brid.

22

BRID: Gladly, Gregory.

MISS CARSTAIRS: Please call again when you're in
the area.

The smile on MISS CARSTAIRS's *face at their
discomforture is only slight, while the* KIOSK LADY
*is grinning so hard that her nose touches her chin like
a witch's. The* KIOSK LADY *begins to cackle as*
BRID *and* GREGORY, *shaken, but moving together,
their dignity intact, walk carefully to the front door.*
GREGORY *opens it for* BRID. *Unobserved by them,
the* MYSTERIOUS COUPLE *have appeared at the
head of the stairs and are also grinning hugely at*
BRID *and* GREGORY's *retreat. As* GREGORY *opens
the door, rain gusts through it even though sunshine
is still beaming through the great windows inside
the house. They are outside in the gloomy weather
once again, and a gust of wind snatches the door from*
GREGORY's *hand and slams it shut. It is thundery
outside the house. Great purple clouds pile hugely
in the sky.*

BRID: Let's walk a bit.

GREGORY: It's going to rain.

BRID: Let it.

He takes her arm. She does not object.

GREGORY: What a funny lady.

BRID: The ticket lady. Did you see? She had tufts of hair
on her ears.

GREGORY: Hypertrichosis. Hypertrichosis partialis. Not
uncommon.

23

BRID: I know. But most people shave it off their ears!

They laugh together at that, and stroll close together through the topiaries of the lawn. BRID *still clutches her postcard.*

BRID: She said there was a horse. Perhaps it's the great great great grandson of Miss Carstairs' little stallion in the picture.

GREGORY: I expect they've got a regular stable of them behind the house in the mews.

BRID: Look! There's the little horse in the paddock over there. Somebody's left the gate open, it's coming across to us. I wish I had a lump of sugar or an apple.

GREGORY: Let's pull up some of this long grass, offer it to Miss Carstairs' little horse.

As BRID *offers the little horse a tuft of long grass pulled from beneath one of the bushes, the animal draws back its lips and whinnies at her* **exactly** *as the doorknocker horse whinnied to greet her before.*

GREGORY: Whoah, boy!

BRID *looks startled for a moment, then pleased.* GREGORY *strokes between the horse's ears,* BRID *offers it more grass. The two humans enjoy making up to the vital and lithe little animal. It watches them with large eyes, blows delicately through its nostrils, takes alarm and gallops off. They are disappointed that it has gone. They stand holding tufts of grass.*

GREGORY: If that thunder breaks, we'll be drenched.

A breeze starts up, the trees stir the air with their
leaves. BRID *and* GREGORY *look at each other,*
then move forwards to embrace. A sudden clap of
thunder and a bright flash as they touch. The two are
thrown to the ground. They lie there stunned, not
moving. BRID's *postcard lies face downward on the*
grass, near her hand. GREGORY *sits up first.* BRID
stirs. She has cut her forehead on a stone in the grass
as she fell.

BRID: That was lightning. We've been struck by lightning.

GREGORY: We'd better get out of these hedges. Come
on. Back to the house.

BRID: No, not to that house. Not to Miss Carstairs.

GREGORY: This is an emergency, doctor. We're lucky
to be alive.

BRID *dazed, with a trickle of blood on her forehead,*
quickly picks up her postcard from the grass. They
run back quickly across the lawn to the sound of
deafening thunder-peals. Just as they reach the shelter
of the porch, the rain falls in a sheet. GREGORY
pushes the door open. For an instant the scene that
greets them is **exactly** *the same as the first time we*
saw this interior. Woman sitting in kiosk. Couple with
woman grinning over her shoulder at top of stairs.
GREGORY *glances back to help* BRID *across the*
threshold, she is afraid to come in. When he looks
again, the couple at the top of the stairs have gone,
and MISS CARSTAIRS *is standing in the middle*
of the hall waiting for them silently.

GREGORY: Miss Carstairs, I think we ought to call
a truce, we're very sorry we were rude to you but

we think we had some cause. We'd like to shelter.
The weather is very bad outside and would you
believe it my fiancee and I have just been knocked
down.

MISS CARSTAIRS: Knocked down?

GREGORY: By lightning, Miss Carstairs. We've been
struck by lightning in your grounds and I'm not
a lawyer but as a doctor I can say that that could
have had some very serious consequences indeed. My
fiancée has unfortunately sustained a slight graze on
her forehead from some stone as she fell, but
otherwise we're uninjured. But we're very, very
shaken Miss Carstairs and while begging your
forgiveness for the incident a minute or two back
we'd be more than obliged for the opportunity of
a brief rest in the hospitality of your house and
possibly a sweet cup of tea.

MISS CARSTAIRS: **Lightning**, Dr Treviles? You've
found some lightning in my garden when you
couldn't find any on my postcards? I find that hard
to believe. And in such clement, I think I may say
radiant weather too.

*She gestures to the windows through which the
sunshine still streams.*

BRID: There was a little horse too, in the paddock, and
he looked just like the little horse in your picture on
my postcard and we fed him and his breath smelt so
wholesome, just like the breath of the whole garden,
just like the smell of the whole fresh garden in the
breeze that came just before... Gregory?... the
lightning... so bright... it knocked me out I think...
I can't remember... bright... blank... such a dazzling
darkness...

26

MISS CARSTAIRS: Surely not too bright for the
intelligent Dr Hare I trust. And a little horse too,
straight off the postcard. And even some blood, on
your own forehead, where you couldn't see it,
however hard you looked at the postcard. It was just
underneath your skin all the time, wasn't it, Dr Hare.
And shall I go up to my picture to see whether you
have stolen my horse from the painting, Dr Hare?
My horse and Gainsborough's. There are no horses
kept in these grounds nowadays Dr Hare, we Tory
landlords can't ride to hounds, we can't afford horses
any more even though my painted horse is insured
for fifty thousand pounds, which is more than your
combined practices as doctors is worth, isn't it,
Dr Hare? You must come upstairs with me Dr Burke
and Hare for I suspect you of stealing my horse from
my picture and carrying it off out of my house.

*She is suddenly dressed in full scarlet hunting rig like
the young* MISS CARSTAIRS *in the portrait and she
has the smear of blood across her brow and the fox's
brush in her hand. Grinning like a fox she snatches*
BRID's *wrist and makes as if to drag her upstairs to
confront her with the missing horse, but when* BRID
*resists, dabs with the bloody end of the fox's brush
at* BRID's *already-bleeding forehead.* BRID *with
a quick effort breaks free, runs to the door, tugs it
open and escapes.* GREGORY *holds his ground for
a moment but then* MISS CARSTAIRS *grins whitely
at him with an even more ghastly affability and raises
her right hand again – which now holds a riding-crop.
This is too much for* GREGORY's *nerve – he finds
himself on the porch clutching* BRID *– there is
howling laughter from inside cut off suddenly by
the door slamming again. The echoes die away, and
there is only the sound of the hissing rain. The two
kiss in the shelter of the porch. They are very shaken*

27

by these events, but feel they have each other. The
rain slackens, and they walk out and get into the car
— then GREGORY *remembers and gets out to try*
and loosen the hood on BRID's *side.*

BRID: Gregory, don't bother. It's all right. Truly it is.
I give in. I don't mind getting wet. After all that it'll
be a relief. Nothing much else **can** happen now. Get
in, Gregory dear. Let's go home.

GREGORY *desists with the hood, and they drive off.*
They pass the gates. The notice for CARSTAIRS
HOUSE AND GROUNDS *is now broken, the paint is*
cracked and the letters are illegible. BRID *sees this*
but it doesn't bother her any more. They turn right
at the gates, back the way they came. A little way
along the road we see that a car has pulled up. It is an
open tourer, like theirs, but a modern one. The
occupants are quarrelling and the man is tussling with
the hood. He raises his hand to strike the woman, but
GREGORY *hoots his horn as they bear down on the*
stalled car, and the man turns his intended blow to
a sheepish greeting as BRID *and* GREGORY, *tooting*
happily, gleefully sweep past.
The rain is beating into BRID's *face as they drive,*
washing the blood from the cut on her forehead into
her eyes and then into her mouth. Her tongue licks
out of her mouth to taste it. Then the cut begins
to fade away as we begin the reverse transition back
to the bedroom, through the stages (as before) of
being in bed, driving along, of driving along in the car
naked or in their nightclothes, of lying tucked up in
bed in their car-clothes, of sitting tucked up in the car
in the bedroom, until we are in the ordinary bedroom
again. This sequence might be interspersed with shots
of BRID *riding a little horse, dressed like* MISS
CARSTAIRS, *to the sounds of hounds and a*

28

huntsman's horn, or of BRID *riding on top of*
GREGORY *making love — the suggestion is that they
are love-making, but well and vigorously this time,
and that* BRID *is taking a more active role. There are
pictures of the sun breaking through the cloudrace
and Carstairs House like a great airship moving off
inside the thundercloud amid peals of thunder and
lecherous laughter. These might fade into* BRID
laughing her pleasure with GREGORY.
*At the end we have quiet in the bedroom, the
windows are dark, the couple are sleeping in each
other's arms, we explore this peaceful scene, then we
close up on the table by the bed, where* BRID *has
propped her postcard. It is clearly visible under the
lamp: it shows* MISS CARSTAIRS DRESSED FOR
HUNTING. *But now the fresh blood shines on the
forehead, the fox-tail is held up in the young woman's
hand, and out of the window in the postcard the
lightning shoots jaggedly down on to the painted
landscape. As we watch it, it brightens slightly, and
a peal of thunder echoes in the distance.*

IN THE COUNTRY OF THE SKIN

A RADIO SCRIPT

PART ONE

(Music)

VOICE: White door.

VOICE: Black door.

VOICE: White door.

VOICES: White door. Black door. White-black door. White-black. Black-white. Door.

(Sea noises)

VOICE: Out at sea
Waves flee up the face of a far sea-rock,
    it is a pure white door
Flashing in the cliff-face opposite,
Great door, opening, closing, rumbling open,
    moonlike
Flying open on its close.

VOICE: Black door.

VOICE: She wears the long series of wonder-awakening dresses.

VOICE: The fishskin dress.

VOICE: The seamless dress of pearl with the constellations slashed in its dark lining, open it and you see the night sky.

VOICE: Each night of the year she is different.

(Pause)

VOICE: She plucks a narcissus and the underworld
          opens in the water-meadows. The three girls have
          been playing in the water. Their blue dresses are wet
          and sparkle as they run. An old black woman sits in
          a cave. She sits just out of sight.

VOICE: Black Teresa plucks a narcissus and the ground
          opens. The turf rears back like a caterpillar. It rears
          off black earth. The earth rears like a tidal tsunami
          off granite, which sparkles like the stars. The granite
          shears like a lid, straight and cutting. She descends.

VOICE: She descends into a red room to inspect the
          pictures, which are always fresh.

TERESA: I smell shearing rocks. Where is the red room?

VOICE: She smells shearing rocks. Some of them give
          off an odour of genius.

VOICE: Others smell of strawberries.

VOICE: This one smells of a great chorus.

VOICE: This one of her mother's black face.

VOICE: This one of a wink.

VOICE: This one of a stag.

VOICE: This one of a moth.

VOICE: This one of the houses of Parliament.

VOICE: This one of Mary Stuart's raw stump.

34

VOICE: This one of the migrations of swallows.

VOICE: And there are too many things to see.

VOICE: Too many things to touch.

VOICE: Too many things for one skin to achieve.

VOICE: Especially a black one.

VOICE: And the white door shuts.

TERESA: I MUST GO BACK TO MY STUDIES. I MUST
          GO BACK TO MY STUDIES AGAIN. AGAIN.
          AGAIN.

(Pause)   (Music out)

SANDY: This is the story of her studies. It is a true story.

(Music)

TERESA: (sings)   And in each hair is a fountain
                    And beneath each fountain a door
                    And through each door a river
                    And in each river a tree
                    And hanging in each tree a worm
                    And round each worm a bracelet
                    And in each bracelet a light
                    And in each light a horny skull
                    And in each skull a wand
                    And in each wand a scroll
                    And in each scroll a flock of wings
                    With a squad of dew in each feather
                    And a lover in each dew
                    And in the lover a battle
                    And in the battle hidden fountains
                    That break within each hair.

SANDY: This is the story of Teresa's studies. It is true.
Enchanting at first. Then there is noise. Then there is
noise again. And then there is silence...
(sings off-key)   And in that silence enchantment
grows, again.
Teresa began her studies with the man she loved.

JONAS: A matter of opening doors and travelling
pathways, Teresa.

TERESA: Yes. I want to hear more about that.

JONAS: In your dream, the brown sugar you were
eating...

TERESA: That is disgusting!

JONAS: Brown **sugar**. That's why your dream made it
brown **sugar**.

TERESA: Well, continue. I cut it up into four equal slices.

JONAS: It's the same stuff, however many slices you
cut it up into. The four slices are the four abilities
of your nature, the four Zoas.

TERESA: If you say so. I follow.

JONAS: Well, that's one door open, one path clear.
When I sat you down in the mud in your white dress,
you said it made you feel like a goddess.

TERESA: I was surprised and divinely insulted. If we'd
gone on we could have been completely alike. Two
slippery clay statues in the sculptor's bin. Not black

and not white. You did something that started to
erase the difference. So it's a path... even that. I think
we are as full of pathways as veined marble.

SILAS: I am the statue, and I begin to breathe.

(Pause)

SANDY: Teresa began her studies with the man she
loved, and he became a casualty of them. His name is
Silas. When he is being clever, he is called Jonas. But
otherwise he is Silas. There were other casualties. I to
all intents and purposes, disappeared. There was
a man called Tomas — more of him later — who lost
certain powers his friends believed he possessed.
Teresa's studies with Silas-Jonas began with
conversations, like the one you have just heard. Often
these were about her dreams. Sometimes though he
sent her on missions.

JONAS: Go into the wood and find the brightest thing
you can see there and then come back and tell me
about it.

TERESA: I am walking between the trees. I want Silas
to be pleased with me. The first thing I notice is
a pond. It is bright, and shines to me a long way off
through the trees. I come up to the pond. It is so
bright! I kneel down and strip off the thin skin
of reflections, roll it up and put it into my pocket
to show Silas. The water's new skin reflects with
more brilliance and better colour! So I kneel down
and pick off this new skin and put it in my pocket,
throwing the other skin away. But the colours of the
newest skin are without equal! So I will take this new
skin to him instead. In due time I empty the pond in
this manner. All that's left is a hole in the ground,

37

with a few fish slapping about in a quag. Poor fish!
I take off my shoes and descend into the mud. It
comes up to my knees.   *(Sounds)*   There!
All the fish are captured. I put them in my skirt all
wriggling and hopping, and climb out. I look for
where the torn scraps of reflection have settled among
the trees. I slide a fish into each one. Now I will go
back to him.

JONAS: What is that wet patch on your skirt!

TERESA: But his suspicions were drowned in amazement
as I unrolled the tapestry of colours for him.

(Pause)

SANDY: They enjoyed sexual fantasies too.

(Music)

JONAS: Three pairs of hands appear. Hands only. One
pair plays the violin,   *(Music)*   another lights the
candles, the third adjusts my cravat.
She arrives in a straight dress of white silk. She praises
my servants: admires the music, the service, the
valeting. I clap my hands.   *(Sounds)*   The meal is
served.   *(Sounds)*   One pair of hands carries in the
meat, the second whets the knife, the third carves.
A cycle of sonatas on the piano commences.
(Scarlatti)   The meal completes itself, in great
harmony. The first pair of hands brings in a little
table, the second settles us in chairs, the third carries
a wand in its left hand and taps the table.   *(Sounds)*
At the first tap the black wood turns brown. At the
second green. At the third tap grass prickles through.
A little lawn has sprung over the table-top, smooth as
a billiard-table. A stream creeps across from left to

right, crystal clear and gently purling.
A trapdoor opens and a gold-sheeted bed set in an
arbour of roses rises gently into view. The wand
traces out a second trapdoor in the turf. It opens and
a dazzling light pours forth. Up out of the light step
two figures, hand in hand. They make their way to
the bed. Lying on the bed they slowly remove each
other's clothes. Their faces are replicas of our own.
Teresa spills her coffee, which traces an ugly trapdoor
on her skirt. She struggles to rise, I struggle to rise but
two pairs of hands prevent us.
I feel a moisture in my groin, the curled stain in her
lap shines bright and black.
Our heads are held and we are compelled to watch.
The small figures arrange themselves into sexual
arabesques. These postures have names. The couple
becomes the Wailing Monkey Embracing a Tree, and
they come with tiny soprano cries.

(Children's voices)

They become the Bamboo Altar, the Muscled Flower,
the Spanish Festoon and the Precession of the Gills,
in rapid succession.
I see at the corner of my eyes white-gloved fingers
keeping Teresa's black eyelids open. The hands
gripping my head are gloved in black, like an
undertaker's.
Suddenly the table vanishes and all is dark except for
dawn seeping around the curtains.

(Music out)

SANDY: They had frequent bitter arguments.

JONAS: ... there's no such thing! A triangle is an
           abstraction, a word, a slice merely, the mark of a wind
           on water.

TERESA: A slice what of?

JONAS: And there's another thing. Not only is a triangle
a nothing. One triangle is less than nothing. A triangle
only begins to have meaning as one of a pair.

TERESA: If you say so.

JONAS: So a triangle is a slice of a cave or a snail's shell
or a whirlwind or a volcano (that geological
maelstrom) a womb or a lily or a penis.

TERESA: I thought that was coming.

JONAS: I refuse to be distracted; none of these things
acts on its own behalf. The whirlwind ransacks the
land, the cave shelters the spring, the volcano teaches
the sky thunder. When the one acts, the other attends;
when the one is emptying, the other is filling; when
the one is light, the other is dark, and shadows of
light growl in it, streaks of dawn; and when the one is
female the other is male, and the male never rests
until he becomes female nor the female until she has
become male.

TERESA: Here are some ribbons for your hair.

SILAS: (humbly)   Thank you.

(Pause)

SANDY: Often he showed off to her...
He reached into her black handbag and took out
a white archangel by the hair, which crackled in
his grasp.

(Electrical crackling)

JONAS: Blast! That's not what I was looking for.

SANDY: His hand throbbed with white pollen. He wiped
           it clean on a trouserleg. Then he reached into her
           handbag and took out the public hangman, who was
           praying.

               (Voice gabbling Latin prayers)

JONAS: (hastily)   No you don't want him.

SANDY: So he quickly replaced that item. Without ado
           he reached into her handbag again and pulled out
           a large squid beating snare drums.

               (Drums)

JONAS: That's still not right.

SANDY: He reached into the quaking purse and took out
           a red madhouse *(Crazy laughter)*, it laughed crazily
           as he shook it, so he put it back. Then in rapid
           succession he brought out a shipwreck with mariners,
           *(Storm noises with voices crying: "Belay there, you
           lubbers! Box the foresail capstan!")* a faithful spouse
           at the loom *(Rhythmic loom-banging)*, a jar of Loch
           Ness monster tadpoles *(Splashing and hooting)*, an
           emblem of virility in the form of the trinity, and this
           (Hissing) was nearly red-hot, four new pence *(They
           ring on the table)* and a thunderstorm which drowned
           their voices. *(Thunderstorm)*

SANDY: And in due course they joined a magical society,
           in which they quickly gained high rank, for Teresa
           had much talent, and they were lovers. Teresa has
           most of the talent, but it is untutored; Silas has most
           of the rank, being a man of immense Will. This Will

he called by his magical name: Jonas. Two men in one
white head and one black woman; two men wearing
a mutual white skin, spiralling with the black woman
through their coloured visions together. Visions
created in them by the one energy of many names:
love, sex, dreaming, perversion, art, womb, geology,
god, justice, cruelty, atomic hydrogen, galactic milk,
celestial holography, menstruation, poetry, magick.
The energy that steers the world like a hurricane
whirlwind and most people hide their heads in their
cellars, which only a man or woman of immense Will
can ride with cruelty and imagination, and must not
relax in his riding for an instant, sleeping or waking.

(Music. Magical ceremony: gongs,
pipes, small flutes, drums, etc.)

SILAS AND   (chanting in unison) We are a man with
TERESA: a peeled stick and a whistle. A piece of red
            wax leaps out of our ear and becomes a red fox on
            the hillside. Our snot is a fat black toad. We keep him
            in a tobacco-tin and add to him. He rumbles in our
            overcoat. We have other friends too slimy and deep
            to mention. If you pick our flowers at night, if you
            steal from us, you will meet them. We have made
            a badger and a donkey from our hair and whiskers.
            When we pull the strings the cattle low. On the
            hillside, among the foxes, a cloud passes through
            the bones of two animals that died fighting each
            other, and us.

JONAS: (sotto voce) It's Shrove Tuesday, so I take the
            throne of swords. That Practicus with the counter-
            tenor is terrible. I must replace him. We ought to have
            a mezzo-soprano there. Where is my athame? Here is
            the rod of manifestation. I lift it by the female end.

TERESA: No longer dead, the grass grows to music. *(Orchestra tuning)* I play the lush brown violin strokes. *(Orchestral effects)* The forest springs up, swaying. Pizzicato gives me frogs, dotting the marsh. Trombones pump daffodils into it. A roll of snare-drums announces swallows. My baton drips with the one compendious note. I am conductor. We are playing a piece called One Brief Afternoon on A Flat Beach of Waves *(Chord modulating A flat to G major)* with that Girl the Colour of G Major Who Knows the Score.

SILAS: The veil wavers, and I am choosing cabbages. Now it is a crystal I am warming between my hands. I spit on it, though that is not allowed. There's my name forming in the crystal S–I–L–A–S.

JONAS: I will break it like sugar into my other name J–O–N–A–S. The furry dark smell of Teresa! It crumbles J–O–N–A–S.

SILAS: S–I–L–A–S is forming again. Now I am choosing cabbages. Put the crystal down, gently. Howl at it.
OOOOOOOOOOOAAAAAAAAEEEEEEEEEMMMMM.

JONAS: The crystal is cloudy, it crowds with knots, it clears.

TERESA   (in unison) As we rush out, the splash of
AND SILAS: frosty dawn against us is a snowy ruffled shirt and a pair of nankeen trousers we had thought were waist-high buttercups. The sun rises. A red waistcoat now, and a green bowtie, eyes as big as saucers, and frizzled hair. We open our golliwog mouth to taste the sun with our sliver of blue sky. We shall stay here for our raven-tailed coat and our bristling hair of starlight.

TERESA: AAAAAAAAAAEEEEEEEEAAAAAAAMMM.

SILAS: Teresa! I've nicked my finger. Here. On the
         sword. The blood-answerer looms! The blood-bead
         grows galaxies!

TERESA: Into the fire. The fire. The brazier.
         Here. Cauterize the blood.

SILAS: AAAAAAAAAAIIIIIIIIIIIIIIIEEEEEEEEEE.
         (He sobs)

(Music out)
(Pause)

SANDY: Now you know what Silas (whose will is called
         Jonas) and Teresa are doing behind the walls of the
         world. But I? Well, call me the Sandy-haired Man.
         I used to be a person of no consequence, of no
         account whatsoever, until they were cruel to me. But
         Silas and Teresa taught me to be small, and this made
         me great. In a small way, that is to say. I went to
         Silas—Jonas first of all, to study, as Teresa did. Jonas
         received me in a plush-lined cellar, and listened as
         I told him how sidling and insignificant I had always
         felt, how I had done all I could to improve myself by
         correspondence courses, how I stood up to the boss,
         and lost my job; how I took the Charles Atlas course,
         and dropped the world.

JONAS: Hypnotism is the only answer. Before you can
         grow great, you must become small. Lie down, please.
         You are tired, your eyes are drooping, your lids are
         heavy, you can hear me and only me and only my
         voice and you shall see and feel what I tell you to see
         and hear and feel...

44

*(Music. In the following sequence
magnified sounds of champing,
tinkling, wallowing, crawling, etc.)*

JONAS: I sent him into the wine-glass to listen to the
dinner-table conversation.
I prodded him into the apple-burrow; I told him
to take out his pin-dagger as soon as he heard the
maggot chewing. I gave him a bath in a walnut-shell.
He made a table-salt necklace, piercing the crystals
together.
He screamed when he fell into the mustard. I rolled
him clean on a piece of bread. He ran from the reek
of my steak like the evisceration of an elephant;
I gave him a cress-leaf fan.
He got drunk in a grape. I found him snoring like
a fly on his back in the punctured skin.

SILAS: It was after I had eaten the blood-orange that
I missed him.

(Pause)

JONAS: Now we will repeat Dr Freud's famous
experiment. I will touch you with various objects,
and you will tell me what you perceive.
A drop of water on the brow.

(Fanfare)

SANDY: I am the Emperor of Abyssinia, and the plumes
wave in my crown.

JONAS: Tickle the nostrils.

(Parrots)

SANDY: I am a creeper growing sideways in the rain-
          forest and I support forty clumps of berries with
          great joy!

JONAS: Eau-de-cologne on the back of the hand.

(Strauss)

SANDY: I am dancing among my fellow-officers in the
          ballroom, in my arms a white muslin lady.

JONAS: The note of a tuning-fork.

(Note modulating to jungle noises)

SANDY: I am thigh-deep in mud. On the bank in front
          of me many alligators in unison open their jaws.
          A foul wind blows!

JONAS: A torch-beam on the closed eyelids.

(Greater fanfare)

SANDY: I am Suleiman, attended by genii like bars of
          iron light.

JONAS: A torch-beam travelling the throat.

(Drum roll)

SANDY: My shirt is deeply open in la toilette
          de guillotine.

JONAS: A hot poker close to the eyes.

SANDY: I am early to greet the sun. Teresa behind me
          begs me to come back to bed.

46

JONAS: That's his game is it! Very well.
           An edge of paper across the Adam's apple.

*(Drum roll: snick of guillotine and gasp from
the crowd, wordless song from one
of the children's voices receding)*

SANDY: Jonas has cut my throat! My head swims the
           river, singing as the sky grows dark. The water dries
           to a silver web, my head is caught like a fly. Teresa
           comes loping along, she wears a terrible spider-mask
           and picks my head up like a crumb of bread. She puts
           it in Jonas' lap.

(Chord)

TERESA: Here he is, Silas.

JONAS: He is weeping with gratitude.

SANDY: And Jonas fastens me to the chain around his
           neck. He puts me to his ear and I whisper praises.

(Pause)

SANDY: But you see, I find life full of interest. There is
           a radio-set here which is connected to the muscles,
           bones, penis and brains of the great magician Jonas—
           Silas himself! I love twiddling through the stations
           and writing down good phrases. For example, listen:

*(Music. Radio tuning noises and the
children's voices announcing
the following:)*

VOICE: A grandfather clock which is a runic sequence.

VOICE: A vase full of cool cheese.

VOICE: A long read of a book in terror and pain.

VOICE: The grass lawn and its lighted staircases.

VOICE: A laughing bird with a painted throat.

VOICE: A fly's cunt modelled in brass and set in a ring.

VOICE: The girl with no scars steps out of her coffin.

VOICE: The skidding cheer of the fairground audience.

SANDY: And that is how I write my poems. But, look,
he's not so hot, is he? He's less of a whole man than
I am, comfortable in his neckstone. And the world is
so large and vivid since I am shrunk to a point. It's
not as though I were shut up, either. Shortly after
I arrived, I discovered a black door at the back of the
neckstone. I open it, pass through... and here I am in
the large amethyst of Teresa's ring. At the back of her
stone there is a white door that leads me back to Silas'
neckstone. Standing in Teresa's ring, I swing like
a pendulum as she cuts up meat. Her knife descends...
wheeeeeeeeeaaaaaaaaammmmm. Sometimes when
they make love I am standing here, watching out
of the faceted window, stroking my cock as they
stroke each other, until all three of us come together
like one person! Oh! Oh!

(Verdi: Dies Irae)

End of part one   (Music out)

48

PART TWO

TERESA: Hush, Tomas is coming.

TOMAS: Well now, we're quite private in here. You can
tell me your troubles. The cottage, I think you said?

JONAS: Stuff it! *(Laughs and exits)*

(Pause)

TERESA: That was a stupid thing to do.

SILAS: The room was shaking with envy as I walked in.
So the only thing to do was to spit on Tomas' carpet
and get out. He's only a man.

(Pause)

TOMAS: The second interview was more successful.

*(During Silas' next speech there are
no sound effects)*

SILAS: It is as if someone constantly swung the handle
and changed the plots. It is as if the whole peninsular
swung on hinges and clicked into a new setting. It is
as though the rocks became radium and the air
crackling nylon. I can feel your personality in your
handclasp, it is boiling silver in the grip of your
fingers. And your white hair leaves streaks in the air.

*(Tomas' next speech following is full
of sound effects, in contrast to
the preceding speech.)*

49

TOMAS: Whereas I, Tomas, I fare well. I hear the trumpet
         unfurling on the wind, the empty water-bottle by my
         bed fills tinkling to its brim; with a thin high singing
         from the millions of boulders grinding, the mountain
         bends, plucks a bough of blossom from the orchard
         and places it on my bedroom windowsill. Its warm
         perfume drifts in, for a moment I hear that white
         perfume play a snatch of a gavotte on bells, then
         a whirlwind forms, a slim whirlwind that marches up
         and down the ranks of apple trees which have that
         instant swiftly come to ripeness. It plucks them and
         fills itself with rosy apples, and like a dancing girl
         carrying fruit on her head, fruit in her skirt, comes
         twirling in through the kitchen pots and pans. She
         piles the fruit deep and ready on the stairs. She sings,
         Apple—Tomas, retired.

JONAS: You're as mad as I am.

TOMAS: Won't you help me then?

SILAS: How can I help?

TOMAS: Tell me your troubles.

(Pause)

TOMAS: I learned how Silas and Teresa, in a peaceful
         time, began living together. Their cottage was on
         a headland, in an oak-wood, a good place, where
         the waves split in two before their prow of rock,
         where the currents revolved in figures-of-eight. The
         name of the cottage was Sheerfin. A glow-worm in
         the sea-night, the comfortable cottage-rooms lighted
         brilliantly in each segment with lamps burning insect-
         oil. Lying in the bedroom that overlooked the sea,
         inside each other, differences of sex vanishing in

50

Karezza, neither black nor white, he in her, one finger
of hers in his mud, they dreamed each others' dreams,
they changed the world, altered the house, controlled
the weather.

They loved to enter the alchemy of the old cottage-
stones. Each stone was a transmitter and a receiver.
You had to be on the alert however. Once Silas found
Teresa in a trance. Her hand had sunk into the stone
up to its elbow. Dreaming she muttered that she was
back in the forest mud, before the stone had been
formed, and partly in the butterfly, and partly in the
flower it was pollinating, both of which were now
a stone fossil at her fingertips deep in the wall.

JONAS: Teresa, how often must I tell you that you
           have to wear your rings on both hands. You have no
           choice but to be what you have become. There is no
           turning back. These rings are your showshoes and
           guides, pitons and ropes in this white world you've
           entered.

SANDY: (gleeful)   The more rings she wears, the more
           doors she gives me.

TOMAS: One afternoon, as she was dressing for tea,
           winding a white rosary round her neck and collar,
           a tall sandy-haired man peered over her shoulder in
           the mirror. She turned swiftly: the room was empty.

TERESA: What are you doing here? Who are you!
           What do you want!

TOMAS: Why was this lean old man walking about their
           rooms as if he owned them? The contradiction in her
           mind was that, as Magus, she needed ghostly approval,
           and could not afford to make ghostly enemies, but
           still she feared him.

51

(To Teresa)
Was it after the disappearance of the Sandy-haired
Man that your house grew terrible? Was it this that
decided you both to come to me?

(Music)

TERESA: I'm frightened, despite my ghost- skill. The
stone caught me again in that instant as water rose in
the walls and spurted from the gaps between the
books, and *(Dies Irae)* faces gaped at me from the
torrent. A sandy-whiskered face pulled itself out
of the stream and limped over to the garden shed.
It pulled open the door and disappeared inside. I felt
a tingling in my ring-finger. Silas called.

(Dies Irae stops)   *(Music out)*

JONAS: Teresa! Are you coming down?

TERESA: Silas, Silas, I've seen him. The Sandy-haired
Man!

JONAS: That is only the man I put in my pendant. That
shed-door leads into my stone. We must never go in
there, for fear of being imprisoned with him. But
I like his nerve.

TERESA: Walking up his own back-passage, like.

SILAS: Laying traps in the mirror.

(Pause)

TOMAS: What a case! Hypnomania and folie a deux!
Dream parasites, dream incest, mutual madness,
a loony duo, twin bonkers, siamese nutters, a batty
binary.

52

SILAS: So saying, the wandering white-winged head full of musical crystals slips back into bed as the first light touches the sky with acid.

(Piano plays, out of tune)

The dawn resembles a beautifully-tuned piano made entirely of sea-shells. It goes ping-a-tunk with acrid notes as the mother o'pearl keys strike. At the aperture, wreathed with true lovers' knots and other cats-cradles, instead of the sun, our ancestors appear. They are not memories and I never dream.

TERESA: This is what I see also between the toast and marmalade and its shadow.

SILAS: You look oddly crumpled as you play, Teresa, and there is a fly walking over your eye. Pay her with tissuey money and let's go.

TERESA: That tune of mine in the cold street has opened up the tightly-wadded ancestor-files, alas.

SILAS: The clouds fill up with inherited faces and you've got the shopping to do.

TERESA: The spectacle wins. The faces above are tearing themselves gently to bits that flutter to the street and line the boughs with white. Look, I am covered with your grandfather's white aunts!

JONAS: Well now, God has unleashed his archives and perhaps we can learn something.

SILAS: The pages shrivel on my palm as I bend to read.

TERESA: Outstare the snow; let the watery white pages melt on your warm eyes.

SILAS: We're in love. We must be. White snowball in your black hand. No snowballing!

TERESA: Look into my snowball. Whose name do you see?

SILAS: J—O—N—A—S.

TERESA: Jonas is million upon million of layered micropages. He is the preoccupied snowman, a white pain with coal eyes and an old hat, and he is grateful to Spring for wasting all his contemplation and turning him into simple wriggling water.

SILAS: His flakes themselves are so silvery, like Hello, like the first words of our meeting. Greed kills them. He and I are the white door.

TERESA: You are the white door.

SILAS: I am the white door. You are the black door.

TERESA: I am the black door.

(Music)
(Pause)

TOMAS: Hypnomania and folie a deux! And mud-fetishism. I've never had a mud-fetish before!

SILAS: Haunt me with erosion, Teresa. You are the black door. You broke free from my arm and jumped down into the mud, and lay in it at your ease, like an odalisque, among its cushions.

TERESA: Darkness like mine falls from every pebble. My rocks rot in the clear rain. I was rock, I shall be rock

again, but now I am too endlessly deep and soft for
thought. I am making endless soil and ponderous
thick earth to wander through, I reflect in my wet
estuaries. I recline at ease among emerald flanks and
winding satin clefts, you will find me in places where
clean ladies don't go, one finger up your tail. You
look out of your window and see me playing with
the dustbins. I look up and see you and smile and
wave and smear tea-leaves down my white skirt.
I wade the estuaries, I shin down cliffs of mud,
I wander through myself, barbaric mire gloats
everywhere.

SILAS: Now tell me the one about the Lady who
Walks...

TERESA: That very dirty black lady allows herself on
certain occasions to be picked clean by the flies, her
numerous allies. They busy themselves about her,
they hum high — I am carrying earth in my rostrum
for her! For her! Slender midges like eyelashes, even
with their soft mouthparts, are glad to manage a grain,
a strand of mucus, a thread of waterweed popping
with animalculae. The big blowfly bluebottle gobbles
it off, crawling pugnose; she is winking with wings
like a blue-sequined skin; then she steps forward out
of this ink-cloud her face shining black that can never
be white, her dress as radiantly white as when she
first stepped into the great mud.

SILAS: More, Teresa, more.

TERESA: They come when she needs them. She is
mistress of flesh-flies. When she's dirty she can be
clean and when she's clean she can be as dirty as she
pleases.

SILAS: Yes, yes.

TERESA: How she loves being dirty and how she loves
          to be clean! And on gold-veined wings, on brass and
          fleshy pinions, with her small brawny flies in their
          jointed horny vestments, her frail grass-green ones,
          her shiny-bun insects, she can replace the earth grain
          by grain into the place where it came from, as if she
          had never wallowed in it.

SILAS: More, Teresa, please.

TERESA: But she may let the earth-dirt be, upon her
          person, for day upon day of her progress, and then in
          the creases of her dress and through her mud-clotted
          hair and in the grimy turban wound round her hair
          the small green things begin to grow, the stubbles and
          fringes of green and the small beards of moss and
          weed. Now she is a black lady of green grass and ivy...

SILAS: Yes, Teresa.

TERESA: And now you have been tied to a lamppost by
          the Army and you have been tarred and feathered.

SILAS: Oh, oh! *(He comes)*

                    (Music climax , and out)
                    (Pause)

TOMAS: I knew what all that meant, of course. You must
          remember that her name, Teresa, means "earth".
          I saw the trouble at once. It was his Will, that he
          called Jonas, that he called Magick, that was making
          them both sick and mad. Right at the beginning there
          were plain signs of the crumbling of Jonas; Teresa's
          ascendancy was growing. I was engaged to cure Silas

56

of Jonas. I have done so, since now he submits to
Teresa. Submitting to Jesus was the old way. Now we
say: Submit to the Anima.
We teach the woman what she is. Jonas began this,
and encompassed his own destruction. We teach the
woman what she is, and we say: submit to the Anima
that she is.
What this is likely to do to Teresa, I don't know. It's
not my concern. Silas, submit to the anima. Teresa,
what does **your** dream say?

TERESA: She is the silver, fish-tailed dancer of the sand.

TOMAS: Nothing more?

TERESA: Nothing more.
Nothing more emerges from the dream. The
sage sits silently, chewing his finger.

TOMAS: There are dreams and dreams...

(Music)

TERESA: The moonlight slowly penetrates him, he is
nearly gone. Quick! I am grabbing an arm, it feels
pulpy. Quick! Tell him a dream.
So I pull my lids down and pretend to fall asleep and
I talk in my sleep about the Anima. Colours flow
back into the old freckled body. The eyes open wide
and begin to twinkle. He salivates with interest. The
white hair over the collar resembles steam escaping
from under the lid of a pot. The eyes blaze. The sun
shines from the glass skull. My closed black face
slowly twists towards his sunlit words and my mouth
opens wide as if drinking them.

TOMAS: I have cured you, now I must withdraw. Help
me up.

TERESA: My dream said: Submit to the Anima. On rising
to his feet, he was no longer the saint. He looked
down at himself, the realization of what had happened
fading with that which knew it in him. Submit to the
Anima. He was a man for whom the morning jug or
pail was a friend, the collie in the corner shop. The
convicted murderer who visited him under guard was
especially a friend. He lived the life of a saint and
a healer, but, truly, he thought himself mad. What is
this, he said to himself, when every little thing, a grain
of dust in a walnut shell, a seaside tavern, looks at me
with a countenance, with a face of such friendly
openness that I have to cry out "Goodday friend!"
Or with a look of such suffering that I must either run
past it or kneel and embrace it. And the people!
Every wrinkle, every quiver, is a sentence that changes
and writes a fresh meaning every second and then
declares itself anew. And he stands fast among those
hurrying congregations of meaning and he says:

TOMAS: I'm mad, I think. Please, can you help me?

TERESA: Sometimes they could. Far too many could
never hear his meaning.
Everybody he treats is faced with the question:

TOMAS: Have you the cure? Have **you** the cure?

TERESA: And the people he treats hand their madness
over to him, expound their mad theories of the origin
of life or how they have been tricked and betrayed,
and he is inspecting it all the time they talk for the
least particle of true madness that would cure him of
his insanity. So one morning, he sitting on the edge
of his bed, warm and open from the expounding of
my dream, in the bare room with the patterned
wallpaper he conversed with because it looked so

miserable, in the room where he listened thriftily and
thirstily to the murderer psychoanalysing him, and
this cured the murderer, I whispered to him the one
tiny grain of true nonsense:
(whispers)
Submit to the Anima.
And he took it up and his mind inspected it and it
ran through his fingers like the hot blood and like
tendrils and it flowered in his prick and bushed in his
eyes and blossomed in his brain and he parted the
leaves and he walked out, and walking out he was no
longer the saint he had been. And as I watched him
go, he was dancing in the chains he couldn't see, all
pain gone. This is how I found a way to cure Tomas,
to exile Jonas, and to live in peace with Silas.

TOMAS: I have told you how I cured Silas of his great
           and terrible Will called Jonas. It was one of my
           greatest cases.

SILAS: Teresa, tell me about **that** again.   *(Music out)*

                    (Pause)

SILAS: Teresa, tell me about the mud again.   *(Music)*

TERESA SINGS: And in each hair is a fountain
                    And beneath each fountain a door
                    And through each door a river
                    And in each river a tree
                    And hanging in each tree a worm
                    And round each worm a bracelet
                    And in each bracelet a light
                    And in each light a horny skull
                    And in each skull a wand
                    And in each wand a scroll
                    And in each scroll a flock of wings

With a squad of dew in each feather
And a lover in each dew
And in the lover a battle
And in the battle hidden fountains
Break within each hair.

(Pause)

SILAS: Teresa, tell me my fortune?

TERESA: Now the black lady steps into the chancel.
Immediately I am among gesticulating figures rinsing
sacred vessels, dropping curtseys at the altar. They are
all men, but they are wearing black dresses like my
skin. I am going to watch the show from the nave,
and I open one of the numerous small black books
giving the order of service. In no time at all I am
bobbing, crossing myself, and apologizing for being
a woman.
This is no good, say I, snapping the book shut and
shouting to the priests who are fiddling with a little
dish covered with a white cloth. They turn their pale
faces and look at me. Before they can look away I lift
my skirt and take a snap of them. This holds them
still. Then I start tickling my tiny penis. The wooden
beams crack and a lump of masonry falls on the altar.
I tickle myself harder.
The church fades away. A holidaymaker I recognize
as one of the priests got up in shirtsleeves and
coloured scarf sidles through the tentflap. *(To the
holidaymaker)* Cross my palm with the silver wheat,
kind sir. Shall I tell you what will happen, or what
you wish for yourself? *(Sotto voce)* The two will not
be so very different, since I am the fortuneteller. So
I tell him what I wish for myself. And a new religion
is born.

(Pause)

TOMAS: *(indignantly)* So much of her theology sounds like gossip!

JONAS: Perched up on the lectern, festooned in her barbaric qualifications, preaching in her mezzo-soprano, she distills lechery into the gospel stories.

TOMAS: And yet she denies it.

JONAS: And yet they flock to her.

TOMAS: All the men see themselves in her stories. Each a Jesus-man in smouldering robes, a crooner with extra-terrestrial divinity.

JONAS: All the women unrepentant Magdalens, goddesses with supernumerary nipples, their short gods awake and their cunts gaping below their short gods.

TOMAS: The whole congregation, including myself, ruminating on the gossip that will be written about me, to be bound between soft leather covers marked "Holy".

(Music)

TERESA PREACHING: Petronella was hurrying from Rome when she met Jesusa travelling the opposite way. "Why, Jesusa," she said, "What business have you in Rome?" "I am going there to be crucified again," replied Jesusa. Petronella was so ashamed she turned around and went back to Rome, to be crucified there. Now Petronella is on her tree, upside-down, it would have been too great a glory to be crucified as her lady was. Petronella's mouth is the great rooting breath. Her lungs turn inside-out with each breath, and ramify through the earth. Her cunt flickers with St. Elmo's fire. The crowds are delighted, laughing and pointing. Between their legs flickers St. Elmo's fire, and they speak with tongues.

(Music out)

TOMAS: She goes too far.

JONAS: She is why women preachers are not allowed.

TOMAS: Silas, what is that flickering between your legs?

(Music)

TERESA PREACHING: You do not understand a twentieth part of what happens to you. You can barely remember the details of the greatest events in your life. You cannot remember being born. You cannot remember your first wet dream. These things are so self evident as they happen, so impossible to remember completely, so rebellious to description. I tell you plainly that I love this man. And what does this mean to me as a woman? That I shall never let him die. That I shall bear his son, or his daughter. And in Goddess' name I believe I mean as much to him. I am the Path, the Door and the Life.

(Music out)

SILAS: Jesus's life was so **charged**.

TOMAS: He was the lover of John, and of Mary Magdalen.

SILAS: My life could never be charged like this.

62

TOMAS: You could say impatiently to an old phoney like me, "Take up your bed and walk!"

JONAS: You get up and hobble off because you're **terrified** of me!

TOMAS: What about the woman taken in adultery?

SILAS: I describe her beauty so exactly to the crowd assembled to stone her, that they see it too, and their clenched hands grow limp from beauty, and the stones fall to the floor.

(Music)

TERESA
PREACHING: What does the virgin birth mean to us in practical terms, as women? Jesus on his cross shows where Goddess-God is and how to obey him-her. To this day the figure on the crucifix leans his head to his right; as the baby is born the head rotates to the right just so. Jesus is retracing his path to the womb, and the cross is the open legs and spread genitals of his mother.
Jesus's grandmother, St. Anne, conceived her daughter immaculately, that is, without sin, without bringing on herself the terrible chaos of labour that stuns the babe into amnesia of the womb. But St. Mary was born without this pain. This meant that she remembered into her mother's womb, she remembered her own growing from coelenterate to fish, from fish to lizard and monkey (and this gave her the power over the animals) she remembered her conception from the explosive union of her father's milk (and this gave her power over the stars) and her mother's egg (and this gave her power over the sun and the moon).
So this meant that she remembered her own womb-growing, and more, that **she could do it by herself.**

So, deep inside her, her cells chose one of their
number to grow and be nurtured into their ideal man,
Jesus, through jellyfish to fish (the sign we sometimes
know Jesus by, the sign of the fish) to lizard to
monkey to man, and this gave him power over the
animals, and moreover she could be with him in her
own womb, and this gave him power over her, and
the stars and the sun and the moon.
Woman, would you not do this for your own man?
Would you not, if he died, give him your resurrection?
Would you not give him eternal life?

(Music out)
(Pause)

TOMAS: Hush, Silas is dying. Teresa, he wants you.

SILAS: Teresa, tell me about **that** again. No, not that.
Tell me about Jonas. Have you heard from him? Did
he write? Please read me his letter.

TERESA: From: Doktor Baron Victor von Frankenstein-
Jonas
The Frankenstein-Jonas Clinic
Karlstadt,
Near Munich, Germany.
My Dear Teresa...

JONAS: *(Fade in)*
My Dear Teresa,
I am writing to you from our clinic's new library.
I am sitting among my patients, just like one of them.
My withdrawal symptoms are gathering above my
head again just like brightly-coloured tree-foliage and
bunches of oyster-shells tied together with slowly-
moving pictures. I have prescribed a nubian vizier to
stand behind me at all times. He lops the growth off

with his scimitar when it becomes too cumbersome. I am a reader here often. The chapters are rapidly-moving beams of light. The letters of the alphabet are like little vials swiftly filling up with a slow clear poison. The dirty secrets lie here in layers, called pages, like oyster-beds. I open one of these books: its cool sinlight pours upwards, and its sea-bed is alight. I believe the chapters multiply afresh each night. I believe that to open a book pulls a string in the librarian's head that starts him cataloguing new books. I no longer flinch at the clear lightning of the dirty jokes. I grow tanned and swarthy indeed in this electrical sunshine.

I shall soon be fit for the outer world, though my hands are as thin and worn as the pages they turn all day. The dinner-bell rings! Half a dozen blueflies that were doing duty as initial letters rise from my page at the clatter, they circle buzzing, and settle in fresh positions. The page now has another meaning which I read with zest, since the more dirty jokes I know and the funnier they are the better I shall be qualified to act and move in the world. Doctor! The only position me and the wife use is on all fours. Doctor: very good, but why on all fours? Patient: how else are we going to watch television? It may happen that I shall die here before I have finished my work. In which case I shall be allowed to dry on my library chair, and my belly will fall open on my spine in many slices which are the natural pages, and then any person coming up to me will be able to read the meaning of my life, and where it is not clear the bluefies and smaller insects will fill it out with a laughable and smutty meaning. The librarian will gilt-tool me with some arbitrary title containing the words "Holy", or "Sacred", and with the one invariable legend: "Beelzebub's Library at the Frankenstein-Jonas Clinic".

So you see, my dear dirty-girl, what pains we are at
to keep ourselves busy at the Clinic.
Are you wearing a soiled dress today? Please write
and describe the stains you put on at breakfast.
Your affectionate friend and tutor,
Victor von Frankenstein-Jonas.

(Pause)

SILAS: *(murmuring)* Frankenstein-Jonas... to say the
least I was impressed by the visit. He must be a most
learned man. I visited one of his research departments,
which is a cross between a greenhouse, a library,
a laboratory, a machine-tool shop and a chamber of
horrors. I noticed a glittering shape in an alcove, like
a pile of silver money or a Christmas tree. It was
a human skeleton modelled out of tinsel. No! said
Frankenstein-Jonas, his hand detaining me, his keen
eyes glittering over his precise lips and clean-cut jaw...

JONAS: No! Do not touch that, Herr Silas. Not yet.
This is a model of all the star-ray convergences that
obtained at my birth. It is alive in its own right. Look
at this portrait...

SILAS: He pointed to one miniature of many hanging
above the long row of tinsel trees...

JONAS: This portrait is the baby of the man you see
before you...

SILAS: He settled his chin more comfortably in his
high stock...

JONAS: We are conceived at the moment that certain
stars shine, and intersecting in that moment's form
they imply us totally. I am the unwinding of this

complex comb, one instant of which you see standing
before you, others of which are glimpsed in the
miniatures and daguerrotypes on this wall. The tinsel
tree-model is made within a light-sensitive solution
of tin contained in a special camera. My father set
the camera to take a picture of the night sky from
his bedroom window in the moment at which I was
conceived. At the instant he felt my mother coming,
he twitched the cape from the camera. As each star
ray travelled through the fluid, its action deposited
a thin rod of tin. Each year my father made a fresh
tree-portrait of the night sky, and had a fresh picture
of my countenance taken. When I die, my son will
take pictures of the night sky, and pictures of me
dying, and of me rotting, and he will watch the stars
that made me no longer converging, but pulling apart
from each other to go their separate ways, creating
new people...

(Music and out)

End of part two

PART THREE

SANDY: As the silver combs drew apart, I walked
quickly from Teresa's ring (kissed by so many of her
congregation, who unknowing were kissing me, since
I was in the ring) into Silas' neckstone. I stand in the
great window looking down at Silas' body. The cock
is limp on its forest, the nipples on either side of me
are losing their colour, darkening from rose into
black. Through the floor I can feel a crackle like
basketwork easing when its load is taken out of it. It
is the crepitation of the cell-walls as their constituents
change, as the heat goes out of them, as the nimble
liquid fat solidifies to lard, as their own enzymes eat
holes in them. The skin is growing whiter, the dark
hair blacker. I lift up my own neckstone. In it I can
see Silas' sheeted figure laid out on the hospital table.
Let me bite the stone off the chain!

(stone-in-mouth   And warm it in my mouth a little. Now
mumble)   into Teresa's ring, through the black
door...

TOMAS: Teresa, do try to drink a little of your soup.

SANDY: Inside Teresa's ring I wind a facet-window down
a little. Can I get my head out? She is lifting the bowl
of the spoon to her gigantic lips.
(He spits, voice clears) There! What a good shot. In
goes my stone right into Teresa's soup. I'll stay a
moment to make sure she sucks it down. Now I can
wind the window up. Bye-bye Teresa! Once I go back
through the new red door I have discovered at the
rear of the ring, I shall not see you for a long time!

(Door closes)

TOMAS: More soup, Teresa. Please try.

TERESA: I can't. I'm sorry.

TOMAS: Will you go on preaching?

TERESA: I shall go into retreat.

TOMAS: But will you go mad?

TERESA: I shall talk to him with all my voices. I will grow him again.

TOMAS: What will you call the child. What if it is a girl?

TERESA: Silas taught me to work the paths. I will grow my Silas for myself and be with him as he grows. It will be like nothing I can expect. There are no words for it. Only process and change. It is as if someone constantly swung the handle and changed the plots.

TOMAS: But if you lose your way on these paths. That will be madness and utter loss. Teresa?

(Music)
(Bring up the children's voices of
blood, bone, heart, muscle, etc.)

VOICE: All things begin to untie themselves. Untied they are water. Water reties itself and becomes him.

TERESA: An initiate is one who can act as a spiral, but I am as puzzled by the sea as I am by churches.

VOICE: The sea, walking arm in arm with the great Jesus.

TERESA: Death is transparent. I tried to unshuck him but

69

he wouldn't come. I watch the clockwork behind his glassy armour.

VOICE: The wind stands on tiptoe.

VOICE: And begins treading out a pearl-dance over the oyster-beds.

VOICE: Purity hides somewhere in the water.

VOICE: Under the bearded and hag-fissured shells.

VOICE: Now the sun ploughs a spiral track across the world's air, winding all the clocks.

VOICE: The earth-clocks are made of glass and metal, or sand in curved female glasses.

VOICE: Of vibrating quartz-crystals in which a pure note is imprisoned.

VOICE: There are clocks mensurated by tuning-forks, clocks that speak the time aloud in verses, clocks that deliver printed horoscopes.

VOICE: The stars are always watching, always working.

VOICE: There are chiming clocks, and bomb-clocks that chime once only, on a quick fuse.

VOICE: There are sun-dials, and clocks that run on oil, tides or electricity, or on the magnetic flux of the earth.

VOICE: There is the pace-maker set in a man's diseased heart.

70

VOICE: There is the gas-flame clock of Bunsen that vibrates to a musical note, and time passes quickly where there is music. There is the clock-note of an instant of the horoscope drawn at conception, and we remember that such is not mere diagrams and letters on a vellum, but fiery sparks in a blackness full of tinkering fingers.

VOICE: There are wave, steam and droplet clocks, rain clocks.

VOICE: There is the joss-stick clock that measures the Geisha's hours, the astronomical water-clock of the Chinese that fills a large mill-house.

VOICE: There is the winter clock of chiming icicles, the potato-clock of sprouting tubers, the fir-cone clock that measures round its dial with cast pollen-shadows.

VOICE: There is the clock that is a spinet full of mercury, and the clock that is a great blast-furnace, whose production divides the year into 100,000 ingots precisely, and whose flares and shadows are visible from the moon on the darkside of earth.

TERESA: *(loudly)*   Bloody clocks!

VOICE: *(as loudly)*   Lady, you have to keep time!

(Pause)
(Sea noises)

VOICE: There are twenty-eight stones lapped by the tide. The tide retreats.

VOICE: A crab emerges from the foot of each stone,

parting the weed with an identical and simultaneous gesture.

VOICE: They march to the fresh stretch of salty sand at the centre of the circle of twenty-eight stones. They mate, with the sound of typewriters.

VOICE: The tide is returning, they retreat to their caves.

VOICE: They have written their page of claw-marks on the sand, as a pack of cards writes its game on the baize table.

VOICE: The tide with its jellyfish is coming like hands to gather up the writing.

VOICE: Teresa chances on the inscribed sand. She leans over the waist-high boulder.

VOICE: She understands the script. The clouds stand still.

VOICE: We stand still.

(Pause)

VOICE: Now the horses come up to her in the meadow.

VOICE: She selects the stallion she needs and rides it into the wood.

VOICE: The stallion becomes her lover, they talk in skin-words together.

VOICE: She is the black lover of the animals.

VOICE: She has read Faust's book without losing her soul.

VOICE: In the wood, she lowers herself upon the
          tremendous kindly sweat of the horse.

(Music out)
(Pause)

TERESA: I have a boat that is always favoured with
          a correct wind. There is a man in that boat who rows
          my way always. I have a purse with a coin in it. Spend
          that coin and another soon takes its place.
          There is an ear I know, it is the ear of the horse I ride.
          If I am hungry or thirsty and I whisper of my need
          into that ear the satisfaction of it will be quickly
          forthcoming. There is a witty head with saliva in its
          beard that is my constant companion. This head will
          joke with me and give me liquor so that I am mad
          with delight and cannot tell the time. There is a hall
          I know and I know the manner of the opening of its
          door. In that hall there are always lights, and a
          banquet. The feasting men turn to me as I enter and
          I am one of them immediately. And it is a church,
          where they divide my flesh and eat and drink of me.

(Music)

          And it is a theatre with scene changing to scene and
          a company of interesting people new and delightful
          to me. It is a drive through my own lands of which
          I am queen, it is a red room I may enter to inspect
          the portraits on the wall, which are always fresh, and
          it is a sewer with rats in it for my enemies.

(Pause)

VOICE: She wears the long series of wonder-awakening
          dresses.

TERESA: Velleity paint, vertigo paint, altitudes printed over my dresses.

VOICE: The seamless dress of pearl with constellations slashed into the black lining.

VOICE: Open it and you see the night sky, each night of the year she is different.

VOICE: Opening of the staircase at the neck, big buttons of bird-skulls.

VOICE: Leather dresses known to be chimp-skin, star-rays combed into a shaggy dress, bone-flounce skirt, turbinal blouse.

VOICE: One dress that shimmers without slit or seam like the wall of an aquarium and a starfish moves slowly on its pumps across her bosom, passes out of view; a shark glides; a turtle rows on, silently, between her knees.

VOICE: And the dress of louse-skin.

VOICE: And another of bird-cries and meteor-noises and declarations of love.

VOICE: A dress of purple jam packed with tiny oval seeds.

VOICE: Another of flexible swirling clockwork running against time.

VOICE: Another of grave-soil that rends and seals as she turns.

VOICE: And another of bloody smoke and bullet-torn bandages.

VOICE: Ticker-tape.

VOICE: Fishskin without slit or seam.

VOICE: A glass bead-game.

VOICE: A pearl.

VOICE: An atom.

(Pause)

VOICE: Too many things for one skin to achieve.

VOICE: Especially a black one.

VOICE: Damaged goods, you might say.

VOICE: She has come a long way.

VOICE: Not far enough.

VOICE: If she comes, we speak with one voice.

(Pause)

TERESA: I see a black iceberg.

VOICE: There is a great deal of music sunk in those
           stones.

VOICE: The iceberg is a rising staircase of black doors
           and white doors stating a formula of great elegance
           and concision.

TERESA: The ghosts are trapped.

VOICE: Ghosts should be free!

TERESA: There's a glint in the black ice.

VOICE: Your ancestors are marching towards you under golden banners.

TERESA: No, it is the sun.

> *(During the following sequence: sound effects. Fragments of a church service, rumble of stones, choirs, rain, organ, etc. superimposed on the sounds of Teresa's orgasm mounting)*

VOICE: There is a fire in the iceberg.

VOICE: The iceflow lurches and we tumble in a heap together.

TERESA: I stand there as the black-white church melts releasing centuries of stored sounds, services chanted, organ anthems, ringing bells.

VOICE: A great bell rings deep in the iceberg, melting it into simple wriggling water.

VOICE: From the bell's mouth a pile of stones drops with a clatter and dust.

VOICE: Now the chimes shake sense into the brick, shiver out staircases and pinnacles, pews and galleries, they toll out a long nave with segments and with sharp clean tones clear wide windowspaces for the sun to shine through and read their bright pictures on the walls inside.

76

TERESA: The new stone hewn out by the bells is bright
and the colour of beach-sound, the woman is a priest
and dressed in white lace warbled out by the small
bells. The service of warm rain begins falling as she
speaks, gathers to torrents as the organ plays and
the choir sings.

CHOIR OF VOICES: The bright water unites our skins.

TERESA: The rain grows plush moss over the pews and
the moss flowers.

CHOIR: Our skins smell the clean chalky presence
of the dark moss.

TERESA: The long series of our wet wonder-awakening
dresses clasps us, our wet hair grips us.

CHOIR: And we clamber naked out of the cumbering.

(Voices and Teresa's coming-cry up)
(Pause)
*(The applechurch sequence following is
quiet, and part of the run-up for
Teresa's second orgasm)*

VOICE: Sun-stones singing.

VOICE: Swimming among the sun-microbes, the
spirochaetes of sunshine, we catch love, badly.

VOICE: Mother Church grows a beard, with saliva in it.

VOICE: It is appletrees and lichen, full of birds and rain.

VOICE: Lichen altarclothtransplants.

VOICE: Applewarehousechurch.

VOICE: Warehousemenandwomenpriests.

VOICE: Full fruitwaftage and waterwaftage.

VOICE: In some applewarehouse churches the fruit grows dry, wrinkled and sweet.

VOICE: And we, the closecongregation of lawnworshippers munch them throughout winter.

VOICE: As naked celebrants we leap into the nave with wooden spades.

VOICE: We smash out at the ciderdecay and it makes us drunk with spiritous bruising.

VOICE: We scour and hoe the building.

VOICE: And we stagger out with light lumps taller than ourselves moulded by groyne and gargoyle, vault and pillar.

VOICE: Edible architecture joyfestering on the grass slopes.

VOICE: We rake out the codling maggots and fry them for meat.

VOICE: They fizzle and squeak in the hot fat. They resemble apple-fritters and we cook them over bonfires.

VOICE: Or we take them home and pamper them.

VOICE: We pamper them like puppies and feed them sleek with apples.

78

VOICE: And we shut them into muslin cages.

VOICE: There they hang themselves up in gossamer and die like husks in the gossamer and hang like twigs.

VOICE: And the dry twig-turds split with tiny soprano cries, with yellow shrieks of joy and the muslin cave is full of speckled moths.

VOICE: Then we shake our white-and-black moths out in the sunshine to fly away.

VOICE: And infect with inebriety other churches.

(Pause)
(Teresa's second orgasm follows. The following sequence of the opening of the ground should be full of sounds: rending rocks, pre-historic animal cries, etc., against the mounting coming-cries of Teresa.)

VOICE: Teresa's bending.

VOICE: She's stooping again.

VOICE: Teresa bends and plucks a narcissus and the ground opens.

VOICE: The turf rears back like a caterpillar.

VOICE: Its underbelly is black as Teresa.

VOICE: It rears off black peat.

VOICE: The peat rears like a tsunami, off granite, which sparkles like constellations. The granite shears like a lid, straight and cutting.

79

VOICE: She smells shearing rocks.

VOICE: She smells the saint-world.

VOICE: Some rocks give off an odour of strawberries as
they shatter.

VOICE: Others smell of genius, or a great chorus.

VOICE: One smells of her mother's face, another of
a wink.

VOICE: And the smells are a river running through
a red hall.

VOICE: And there is a great seat there, constructed
of swords.

VOICE: There is a jostling congregation of smells, like
beards and stags on heat.

VOICE: She sits with the smells, she smells of hyacinths
and moths.

VOICE: She dances in the chains she can't see.

VOICE: There is a shape between her legs which smells
of mountains scraping stationary clouds.

VOICE: Looking down at herself, she is no longer
the saint.

VOICE: This shape of smells runs upwards like roots
and downwards like branches and sees for a moment.

VOICE: And touches for a moment.

80

VOICE: Except there are too many things to see

VOICE: And too many things to touch

VOICE: Unless she comes

VOICE: And   then   we   speak   with   one

VOICES: V   O   I   C   E

(Music out)

*(Receding echoes of the word 'Voice' and
sound-effects down to quiet into which
Silas' voice enters with emphasis.)*

SILAS: *(emphatic)*   White knight takes black queen,
twice.

(Pause)
(Music)

SILAS: She comes like a seashell without a skin, like
warm mud that moves in sections.
She comes like a tree-frog clambering towards some
great fruit, niddip, niddip.
A small acrobat lives inside the flower. The canopy
blooms. Her blouse comes off like the clean paging of
newly-bought books, there is a smell of fresh bread
and a clean active animal with strong teats inside.
She has an underground belfry tolling the bushes,
which shakes the ground.
It is full of shivering moths that fly out and return.
Her knickers come off like opening party invitations
and between her legs pigeons are laying eggs without
shells.
I have lost duration there, and dread, longer than

a man reasonably may. I believe I know white lids
sledding off mossy wells, shearing prisms and silk
splitting far within for me to walk into a red room
and inspect the portraits there which are always fresh.

TERESA SINGS: And in each hair is a fountain
                  And beneath each fountain a door
                  And through each door a river
                  A river made of dew

                       (Pause)

                  I am made of dew, lover.
                  Black queen takes white king. Mate.

                      (Music)
                  *(Bring up sea noises. The crunch
                  of approaching feet over shingle.)*

SILAS: Hello Teresa.

TERESA: Hello Silas.

                       (Pause)

SANDY: I heard of the cottage called Sheerfin in the oak
           wood on the promontory from Tomas. I decided to
           sleep for some nights in the ruined building. I was
           aware that the dead, pressing on the living slantwise,
           pressing upwards from the grains of soil, from the
           atom itself, created strange forms in the receptive but
           fallen brain. I was prepared to relive horrors of the
           death-trauma, and the ecstasies of life re-making.
           These notes owe their origin to my sojourn in the
           ruined house. I am no one remarkable. I have sandy
           hair. In sunlight it shines like old gold.

                     THE END

THREE PIECES FOR VOICES

THE SON OF MY SKIN
BEYOND THE EYELIDS
THE JESUS APPARITION

To Lionel and Prue Miskin

THE SON OF MY SKIN

I

Emperor, Doctor

Emperor: Doctor, how long may a man live after he is flayed?
Doctor: Sir, under proper medical conditions, a man may grow
A whole new skin in a matter of months.
Emperor: Now tell me the most expedient way
Of flaying a man so the skin is unblemished.
Doctor: Sir, there is no way. We would normally begin
With incisions along the spinal column.
Emperor: No, doctor, that will not do.
I must have a skin without blemish
Which is also alive.
You have tissue-culture methods?
Doctor: Certainly the skin can be kept living
Though it would only look authentic if carefully tanned.
I cannot withdraw the living body
Without mutilating incision.
Emperor: That is not true. You have methods
Of plastic surgery that leave no scars. Doctor,
Why do you practice extreme unction?
Doctor: Sir . . . this is not true . . . the priest is called . . .
Emperor: You have a particular drawer in your little black bag
For terminal visits only,
You pack it with ants, and maggots.
You take one of each creature and tweezer it carefully
Into the sick one's hair before taking your leave
Or in his comatose moustache. This is your
Extreme unction, your resignation, and something
Not to be known outside the profession.

You agree?
Doctor: The people would desert us for the priests.
We need this fragment of magic.
Emperor: And my sweat. What about that fragment of magic?
Doctor: Sire, that is true, and secret magic.
Emperor: I have a distillery of virtues for a skin!
The panels of my skin are the rostas of hospitals.
Male nurses bale up my pillaged collars.
Senior physicians bestow pectoral sweat-bottles.
My work should not include magic.
Naturally I am adept in the magical college,
But I hate every turn, every footfall.
To ascend the ladder of lights
With a face like chewed toffee!
These shamans, they are so noisy!
They stampede us grossly.
The brazier-smoke divests like a stripper,
Garment upon garment unfolding on nobody.
The lean incombustible shaman broods, then bounds to his drum,
A grin like a basking toad wings under his long nose,
Maggoty-fingers weaves out the worm-tune,
Whines out of his mouth like a worm-cast crumbling;
Then he chants bloody-muzzles, and with a howl
Battles hobble out of that mouth,
Musketry holes bloom in that voice,
The grimace is a faceful of acid!
The clavicule of a magus is his silent skin.
Then imagination-rhythms crawl through that lantern,
The Book of Shadows
Is skin-written each time freshly.
He discovers the pure pentagram by the way his skin shrinks
Like a statue of silk, silent, and tattering;
Sleep clothes and unclothes him with capillary visions.
I am the night-magus,
My skin is the soundless drum,
Still sweat, sprinting sweat, is its tune.

The acts of the surgeons
Beat in advance there, I dream the cure
My sweat is prescription, it is stolen
Greasy with power, clandestine chamberlains
Unwind their bandages through my night-terrors.
My work should not include magic.
I wish to be flayed.
Doctor: Sire, I could not on my life . . .
You are a man in his prime, in his early sixties,
You have no disease, you are a great prince.
Emperor: On your life, on your wife's, and your children's,
Flay me.
I must have a skin without blemish
Which is also alive. I want
My living body withdrawn through my mouth.
I want to utter
My new skin and body from the mouth of the old.

II

Rustic Visitor

I have been to the city and seen
A marvellous thing. Our new king
Is a man of pearl, a translucent man.
I saw him enthroned, wearing a gold crown.
Water streamed over all his body
And over his closed eyes from under his crown
With his unshod feet in bolsters of foam
(And he, of all men, is naked)
In a golden conduit from which taps fill vases
And multitudes drink. Priestly men
Hand us water to drink from copper vases

That is slightly bitter and salt
And my sight cleared
After tasting that drink. He sits
Like a man-shaped pearl in a golden round
And the many who minister were all doctors once
Ordained now as priests. There is another man
In a simple robe to whom great honour is paid
They call him "The Son of the Emperor"
And his face is unlined and his arms are smooth
Though his expression says
He is a man in his prime. I have never felt
Such feelings or seen such sights: the golden crown
And the pouring water, the pearl man
Shut in a cone of winding water, eyes tightly closed
And lips pursed as in great concentration
And multitudes drinking.

BEYOND THE EYELIDS

Peter Krespel, Jacoba

. . . like thin-skinned insects, which, as we watch the restless play of their muscles, seem to be misshapen. . .

Peter: I am looking beyond my eyelids, Jacoba,
Along the edge where the two halves join,
Where the all-thing is.
Now I see across them
Where you sit
Sipping the cool tart cider
Small buttons dreaming down your white blouse
A million ruffles recording your breath.
Your loose hair gives me cowled religious feelings, of a kind.
Jacoba: I felt cold. Of course that was
You coming over the fields.
I felt like an ill-fitting reservoir.
Peter: The glass clouds, there is a shipwreck in the glass clouds,
The purple hulk shatters
Into a sea of cider, out wings
A white bird
His wings honed to a whisker
Bony and big as a greyhound,
He stoops
Straight into my head!
Jacoba: I'm sorry, the cider
Makes me feel randy
And bad-tempered.
Peter: It loosens my visions, something of yours
Is glittering inside my head, a tiny suede skull
Panting like a rabbit, a boot

For somebody's foot. Two large soft eyes
Buckle it. It grins lacily.
Two fat tears trundle over the welt.
Jacoba: Skulls again.
Peter: There is wheat in a barn
Like yolk in an egg. I love
Honey and yolk and cider
And the colour of your hair.
There skims across that oil-slick speedily
A yellow skull looking out for ribs
It offers a hank of hair for mine.
Jacoba: Peter, can't you open your eyes wide for a moment
And look at me? I didn't laugh at your visions.
It's that you look so silly walking about
With your eyes half closed most of the time.
Peter: If I open my eyes, that switches them off.
How can I not go as far as they take me?
Here comes one for you.
The envelope screams as I tear it.
Thigh-deep in earth, he is so heavy,
From the end of the black hole in the green hillside
Out wades the sulphur-miner with his face
That is earth's answer to the sun's countenance
His eyes are diamond-flasks full of dazzle
He strides up the tree-trunk to his leafy study
He burns in the screaming boughs;
Silverman swaggers out next
Through polished panels
Sliding blue sky and meadows,
Face bright with the metal edges of malice;
Last comes Moon-spittle, sidler,
The things that must have gone wrong
In the depths of the metal to make a face like that!
Among the chain-voiced men he is the chainer
He cannot bear cold
The poor tinner

He bursts to a ball of sleet in the winter cold
He leaves footprints of tin.
You are a honey-haired, honey-voiced
Coward.
Jacoba: It was the way you hit me.
Too much like mirrors, visions.
A blow to the eyes since I wouldn't see
A cuff on the mouth for not talking
A smack to the nose for a stinking whore
Peter: Fire dislikes even numbers, so that three logs
Burn better than two and seven than four.
Jacoba, I told you, you are the visions.
You wouldn't look at yourself.
Jacoba: That means through your eyes, always.
Peter: No. Please speak. Share.
The word for 'joy' in Greek is almost 'voice'.
You think you've stopped giving, but
Just sitting there . . .
I can see through lids half-closed
Meanings that shine from you.
Jacoba: It feels dislocated, it's all clocks
Without their proper bones, watchcases
Full of shadows, nothing is itself,
Butterflies like brittle bats, snails stately
Like travelling reliquaries, spiderwebs
Like fallen constellations, spiders
Barbed like electricity, birds
Of old glass and thistledown, the great bells
Ring like bald skulls of giants
And framed howls, I am the princess
In the ruined clocktower, and in my menagerie
There is a great shining waterspout behind bars.
Peter: The waterspouts rise on a level sea
Like spiral staircases that are also flowers
You sing in that garden, then you cut them down
With a softly-skimming curse

That shines in the dark.
I'll not die with my balls full.
Jacoba: Peter . . .
Peter: I love you . . . you glare on to me—
I see like broken mirrors,
I reflect like a jigsaw.
Somewhere in all that, among the butterflies clustered
And feeding hungrily on the silver bowl of liver,
The red wine swilling in the white bone cup,
Shadows pasturing under the trees—there!
The tiny feet and wings that infest the twilight
With grainy newsreels, the gnats themselves
Grist news-pictures of you under the trees,
Nobody else, just you;
And where in the brown study with the blue ceiling
Time spires only green tines
Out of the silent potato-clock on the log-mantlepiece
The typewriter of rushes
Still wisps out 'Jacoba!'
Jacoba: And you are the seducer
With a precipice in every finger. Peter,
I'll come with you, we'll
Do this together. That bird,
Can you search for it in your head
Where did it fly to?
Peter: Where it perched
There's a door in the battlements.
Jacoba: Open the door.
Peter: A twisting cupboard that reaches
Far back in the wall, stacked
With thin sheets like mica
Jacoba: Pull a piece out, hold it in your hands.
Peter: It glides and glistens in my hands. It is curtains
Over a wall-safe.
Jacoba: Where's the key?
Peter: On the parapet, a great key

Like a peacock of meat and steel.
It is so heavy!
Jacoba: Turn the key.
Peter: The earth opens.
Jacoba: Look down inside.
Peter: I lift my lamp.
It is a winding shell,
Light glistens round me
Spirals down, twists
To a shadowy cusp.
Jacoba: Tread the dwindling stair.
Peter: I push through the tip
Into a glass room
Fire hangs at its centre
I peer through the glass
At a curtained room
I see us there.
You say *look down inside*
And I watch from the lamp
You say *where's the key*
And I watch from the newsmaze,
The folded plantations of print
You say *pull a piece out*
I watch from your lap
You say *where it perched*
I'm in the lace of your cuffs
I watch from the eyelets
I fly up with your hand
You say *precipice-fingered*
I cross a hair long as a river
You say *you hit me*
I squat in a sandy tear-duct
You say *a blow to the eyes*
I sit in them
Like mica watch-towers
You say *skulls again*

I slide down your nostrils
I spread through your bones
You say *randy*
I am between
Your slippery skins like eiderdowns
On tiptoe and working your mouth:
Randy, randy, the cider makes me randy
Like your fidgety mirror, Peter, the greedy jigsaw
Where everything fits, the flinching reservoir
Where water won't rest,
A sledding of lids
All of them mirrors
Plumed waves wind-scorched
With rags of you burning like chiffon foam.
Jacoba: Peter, stop it. That's frightening,
You're frightened . . .
Peter: Say something I didn't make you say, like
Greedy love, I love you,
Your mirror-lined lids—
Grow still, don't flinch,
Let the mirror empty.
Jacoba: Made of stalactite water
The lady in the cavern
Weeps thin lids of stone
Gushes fresh fingernails
Lays new bones down.

THE JESUS APPARITION
An Easter Cantata

Georgina and Silas; Jacey; Maxine and Mortimer

Hell's stones speak aloud as they burn bright for an instant under the passage of God's shining feet.

I *Duet: Georgina & Silas*

Georgina: Fathoms of mire   mud mud mud mud mud mud
Fathoms of retaining mire pointing upwards   endless soil
   pointing upwards, endless soilure
The soft black shadows coming at me   from the rockface
From the boulders, from the pebbles   from all the world's
   beaches
From all the world's sand   from all its dust
Silas: That explosion blinded me to white   the great soft
Touchy whiteness   of her bedroom
   breasty touchiness
Breasty whiteness   like white gunpowder
Roaring at me like red roses like maned tigers
When the white gunpowder of her blew   roses of fire
Georgina: The air is full   of a soft opaque shadow   like
   leather
Over my eyes   I wore white always   am I wearing
   white now?
The dark will not tell me   in the dark like mire
I cannot tell what I am wearing
Perhaps I am wearing mire   I was a careful lady
Silas: The explosion was red as blood   poor lady
   even the midnight

Shines like raw meat   every darkness   has a little
  fleck of red in it at least
A little splash of blood I think   I never see white now
What is white?   What is it for?   Is it innocence?
Describe it to a blind man   Where does white live?
Does it live in some bed?   In some lady?
I was thinking of her delicate white meat as they laid her to
  rest.
She would have the best!   What's in a kiss, a kiss.
Georgina: Careful!   I did not believe in black   I do not
  believe in black.
I am dreaming I am the white madonna.   I dream I am
  the white madonna
And I am sweating black   I wake, and the new black skin
  I have sweated
Covers me, even to the eyes.   Covers my eyes.   Like
  warm soft leather.
Black.
Silas: What's in a kiss, ending in the sapphire funeral?
Beyond the appletrees two fruitful children mark the fine
  sheets of wet sand.
Delicate white meat laid in a sapphire satin in an applewood
  coffin.
She killed herself, poor lady.   I brought her the best.
  White dead white.
Georgina: I think I must once have gone to live in a strange house
that laid itself face-down on the mudflats every night . . . at night
I could never bring myself to open any doors or windows be-
cause of the fathoms of retaining mire . . . pointed mire straining
upwards outside them ready to take me . . . that is why I am in
this white dress so that I'll always know what doors I've opened
. . . except that now it's dark, or I'm blind.
My white breast   covered with white silk   is full
Is full   of white mire of milk   inside my white belly
Is darkness   in darkness   my womb grows   a black
  fruit

Made of mud and grass and hair matted in it and white stones
and teeth
Black hair and white clenched teeth and no eyes for sight
It is a black dress
It is a black dress lightening
There are white streaks in this black dress
It is a dress with scars of dark and white glances
And slow lightning in the night. The mire is clearing.
The lids are parting. The slats are opening.
It is a little damp underfoot. Look at the sunset!
Look at the rooks settling
Silas: A whole continent moves into summer again! I kissed
the black girl, I admit it!
There is a love-book the Arabs have   in letters of gold
Written over the skins of gazelles   we knew it   our
great lion-maned love-books   open
Of their own accord   here is thick turf   thudding with
eland
Children reach for our prey and thank us greedily, we are so
strong we wish to be gentle.
I fucked with the black girl, I admit it.
Georgina: Here's the path through the wood to the bathing-place
with the ruined boathouse, and the tide's down over the mud,
with the sunset on fire in it. All the blacks and heavy browns
have gone, its flanks are purple and blue like electricity, with
emerald clefts in chilly satin channels, like silks and velours spun
out of earth, laid down by the water. The smell! It's thriving:
yeast, and ploughed earth.
Silas: Apples warm and flecked with sunset-blood, the thick
turf
Thudding with apples, a chill through the orchard.
There's a storm coming, it's getting dark too quickly,
A sudden smell of sea through the trees,
Thunder blooms behind them.
Lightning!
Lightning's going to bite, it's going to hit

And where it bites it white-blacks you.
It's going to hit and where it hits it commits surgery!
The shore is cold and pebbly in the rain.
The apples are cold and hard swinging in the storm.
The footmarks on the broad sheets of wet sand fade.
The tide is rising, the black rain is filling the cold sea up.
I am inside the cold cathedral of the rain,
The cold cathedral of the stone. Black.
The red snow drifts down deep and goes out in the frigid
black.

Georgina: The sun drops too fast   the mud slams shut
        the rooks rise cawing   they are sluicegates of night
cascading night   shadows through the trees are coming at me
again   am I screaming or is it the black sun coming back
it has rays of vitriol it is so hot so brightly dark and sharp
oh   but   the black sun strikes down   in mercy
    and fuses me into the centre of a hot black rock

II *Solo: Jacey Eating Plums*

So many souls. Like all the pebbles breeding from all the world's
shores. They say a star has been born for every death since the
beginning of time: astronomers have worked out the actual
numbers. A little girl once told me what happens to people
when they die. 'They turn into mountains,' she said.

Why not pebbles? Or dust. How do you know what's inside
a rock? Or inside the hill across the estuary from my front
door, where the scattered dwellings look more like well-
heads than houses. Or in the holy boulder at Zennor that
makes the woman a witch who climbs on it at midnight? Does
it have a secret nightfall of stars in there? Or solid light? There
is a legend about the standing stones of Stonehenge that, one
night a year, doors open in them. In that instant they light the
plains with sweeping rays. Then the great stone valves rumble

shut again, until the next time. Perhaps all pebbles and stones, mountains and dust are like this. Then on the right evening you might catch sudden grass-growth of light undulating over the beach and under the waves, or at home the sparkle over a dusty table-top, as the infinitesimal city opens its lighted doors.

But I don't believe it. I think stones are hardened people. I think a pebble drops from the corpse when it's carried away. I think there's a little dead scene in this pebble. We hold it a while in a hand or warm it a moment with a bare footfall and it lights up, deep inside. The scene begins to move. A woman shuddering for fear of soil, a man whose dark love has caused another's death, a lunatic still in her cell, a man falling through clouds of anaesthetic in an operating-theatre. They feel again, and as our life warms their stone skins, they move through what might have been. Then we walk on, we toss the pebble away, and all fades. Turned back to stone. Or a few grains of sand.

But I think too of the stones of soft fruit, warmed in the eater's mouth, the small filament inside twitching alight, spat out, maybe on shingle to die, maybe on wet soil, the spike of it rending its own stone portals.

III *Duet: Maxine and Mortimer*

Maxine: I point where the sun should be. God has made me very small. I am smaller than a wavelength of light, so it is always night here, but I still stand pointing at the light I can't see. If you watch my finger you will see it moving very very slowly as the sun sinks. If you stay long enough you will see my finger following the sun as it travels under my feet. I think this will please God.

Mortimer: For me   is   only   whistling darkness
    long long long long
I have been falling in darkness   long long long long

Falling through the earth   falling through the Mohole
Falling   falling somewhere where there are no stars
   whistling darkness only
Falling falling through   whistling mire   through
   whistling more
When will it smash me   so I cannot feel   whistling
   darkness

Maxine: God has made me very large. I am the Pennines. They have been mining my sides and when the sun comes I shall be able to see deep into what they have done to me.

Mortimer: I am whistling water falling   in a mass of
   chuckling caves
Some parts go faster   my waterhead drains away from my
   waterneck
My waterfingers whistle into drops   into spray
Liquors that feel every parting, every meeting   black
   waterfall   through whistling darkness

Maxine: Oh, God has just now made me paper-thin. I am shut inside great-grandfather's big black bible. I am a bookmark. I mark the story of the rending of Jesus' clothes. And I mark the story of the rending of the veil of the temple.

Mortimer: And I am through! I rend the thunderclouds, falling, and they are above me, storm-rafters. The lightning darts, and pauses, looking around itself with solid winding light. I see the sudden-lighted world rushing towards me. Then it stops with a jerk. My parachute stops it with a jerk. And revolves it, slowly. I turn myself, I tilt myself like pouring myself, and I am emerging downwards into all the world, and gravity co-operates, and I have control. Still the light builds crooked towers of itself. It lights me understanding. I see the world, the sights are all laid out before me for my inspection, I am about to be of them. Ah! the light leaps between thresholds of purple. The air is swift and safe against me. The wind rises. I am speeding. I am the white airthing racing through the purple thunderdrome, there are no other skyracers in the big air.

Maxine: And I am this thin bookmark shut in the big bible. And

I mark the story of the great earthquake, and how the stone of the sepulchre was rolled away and the angel of the lord came and his countenance was like lightning and his raiment white as snow and he said, Fear not ye; for I know that ye seek Jesus which was crucified. He is not here for he is risen, as he said. Come see the place where the lord lay. And go quickly and tell his disciples that he is risen from the dead and behold he goeth before you into Galilee; there shall ye see him; lo I have told you and they departed from the sepulchre with fear

Mortimer: The clouds are winning   they are below my feet   purple   they are above my head   purple   they close on me like a mouth   purple   I am in a stomach of purple its rainfall is dancing formication   I am shuddering out of the harness that keeps me in this darkness and I hold for a moment by one hand and I drop

Maxine: and they departed from the sepulchre with FEAR and they denied the sepulchre with GREAT JOY and they departed with great FEARJOY who had come along to depose them and GREAT FEAR imposed mountainous littleness and their JOY WAS GREAT AGONY and they left running and they left falling

Mortimer: through whistling darkness when will the earth strike me so that I do not always feel this falling darkness

Maxine: and they ran into the sepulchre as had been foretold and they closed the great stone and they closed their great stone and as they closed their great stone   the   light   went
     out